GARY VAYNERCHUK'S

101
WINES

1er CRU

GARY VAYNERCHUK'S
101
WINES

GUARANTEED TO INSPIRE, DELIGHT, AND BRING THUNDER TO YOUR WORLD

GARY VAYNERCHUK

RODALE

Rodale books may be purchased for business or promotional use or for special sales. For information, please write to:
Special Markets Department, Rodale Inc., 733 Third Avenue, New York, NY 10017

Printed in the United States of America
Rodale Inc. makes every effort to use acid-free ♾, recycled paper ♻.

Book design by Joanna Williams

Library of Congress Cataloging-in-Publication Data

Vaynerchuk, Gary.
    Gary Vaynerchuk's 101 wines : 1er cru : wines guaranteed to inspire, delight, and bring thunder to your world / Gary Vaynerchuk.
        p.   cm.
    Includes index.
    ISBN-13 978–1–59486–882–5   paperback
    ISBN-10 1–59486–882–4   paperback
    1. Wine and wine making.   2. Vineyards.   I. Title.   II. Title: Gary Vaynerchuk's one hundred one wines.   III. Title: 101 wines.
TP548.V37 2008
641.2'2—dc22   2008008811

Distributed to the trade by Macmillan
2   4   6   8   10   9   7   5   3   1   hardcover

We inspire and enable people to improve their lives and the world around them

For more of our products visit **rodalestore.com** or call 800-848-4735

To my amazing family, I am nothing without you.
Mom, Dad, my wife Lizzie, sis Liz, and bro AJ:
You guys are my heart.

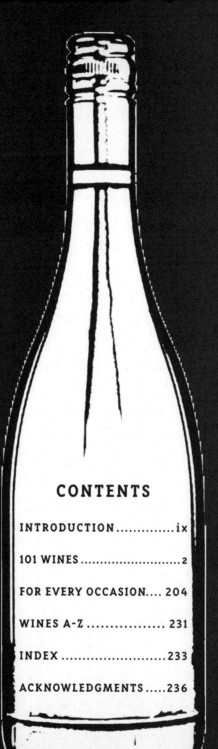

CONTENTS

INTRODUCTION
(This Is Not a Wine Guide)

A lot of people are born into the world of wine. Their families own vineyards or include twelve generations of winemakers. They grow up swirling and sipping wine at the dinner table and inherit cellars filled with dusty bottles along with their trust funds. I am not one of those people. And I'm guessing you are not either. However, even as the son of an immigrant family from Belarus growing up in New Jersey, wine found me. And if you're holding this book, wine has just found you.

To be honest, I resisted the lure of wine. What I was born to be—blessed to be, really—is an entrepreneur. From the moment I could make a pitcher of Country Time, I was selling lemonade, raking leaves, shoveling snow. No season was safe. Then, at the age of 14, I found what I was certain would be my life's calling: trading baseball cards. I'm not talking about swapping a few cards on the playground. I was in the eighth grade and pulling in a grand a weekend, which was a credible income back then and qualified me as Ethel Hoppock Middle School's equivalent of a billionaire.

Unlike many other Eastern European Jewish immigrants, my father, Sasha Vaynerchuk, refused to be contained by the Old World communities of New York. I grew up in Edison, New Jersey, and later Hunterdon County, New Jersey, where, concurrent with my baseball card business, Dad had achieved his own immigrant success by owning and operating two liquor stores—all this despite arriving here in 1978 with no money and no English.

Then my father put me to work at Shopper's Discount Liquors in Springfield, making ice and cleaning shelves for $2 an hour. Maybe I was an atypical 14-year-old boy, but I could have cared less about liquor or beer. And I surely didn't give a rat's ass about wine. All I knew was that all my friends were at the Phillipsburg Mall, my pockets were overflowing with cash, and here I was making ice on a Saturday afternoon for a whopping 20 bucks. It was brutal. The only positive thing about the experience was working with my family. Because more than wine, more than the New York Jets, more than anything else I talk about—which is a lot—I value my family.

My father's store in Springfield was surrounded by affluent New Jersey communities, so there was a well-heeled wine clientele. My duties at the store grew, and I remember when, in 1994, Caymus Special Select 1990 from California was named Wine of the Year by *Wine Spectator* magazine. Droves of people came in asking for this wine. That's when I had a revelation: People collect wine. Suddenly, I realized that a cult Cabernet like Silver Oak was no different than a Pete Rose rookie card. By this point, my passion for collecting included not just baseball cards, but also comic books, Star Wars toys, and now—strangely enough—wine. I put down the *Beckett Baseball Card Monthly* and picked up *Wine Spectator* and Robert M. Parker Jr.'s *Wine Advocate*, which forever changed my life.

Through a combination of passion and genetic predisposition, my father and I turned his local liquor store into Wine Library, one of the fastest-growing wine retailers in America. Winelibrary.com is one of the most-visited wine Web sites on the Internet, and Wine

Library TV (WLTV) has more than 60,000 regular viewers (as of March 2008).

So why write a book, especially when so many wine books already exist? Because this book is not another "guide." It won't help you quickly find a bottle under $15, or offer reviews of 10,000 wines, or teach you to judge wine so you can impress your friends. It *will* help you to create your own story with wine. By reading about and tasting the wines I've included in this book, you'll discover your preferences, train your palate, and pursue your own path to understanding wine. So if my methods seem unorthodox—or downright crazy—it's because I want your discovery of wine to *not* read like a script from some encyclopedic pocket guide. Guides point the way for you. I only wish for your discovery of wine to be as unique, exciting, fun, and full of surprises as mine.

Changing the Wine World

If you're one of the legions of Wine Library TV viewers—the self-described Vayniacs—who faithfully watch WLTV on the Internet, you can probably recite my sign-off by heart, "You, with a little bit of me, we're changing the wine world, whether they like it or not."

Changing the world—even just the "wine world"—is never an easy task. The wine world as it already exists has been pretty good to me, so I'm probably the last guy who should want to see it change. I built my multimillion-dollar business by selling wine. I was Crazy Eddie, Barnum & Bailey, hawking Australia and Spain five years before anyone else saw them coming. It's not that I was a bad guy. On the contrary; I was a great retailer and very good to my customers. But, it was all in the name of business. Now, I'm able to give back. I want to look back on these years and feel like I helped people, and if that takes changing the whole damn wine world, then so be it.

Wine is perhaps the greatest metaphor for life. More than business, or sports, or the proverbial bowl of cherries, the wine world, with its prejudices and misconceptions and stereotypes and darlings and outcasts, is like life. I hope the one thing that's immediately apparent to anyone who meets me, or watches even one episode of WLTV, is that despite my loud, in-your-face, opinionated, "Jersey" personality, I love people. In high school, I never bought into cliques. I had all sorts of friends, from the hottest cheerleader to the kid who had exactly one friend and his name was Gary Vaynerchuk. My approach to wine is the same.

Think about the recent rise of Hollywood darling Pinot Noir. Like a high school quarterback, Pinot Noir is indulged by everyone, almost regardless of the quality that's inside the package. But what happens ten years from now at the reunion? When Pinot Noir, with a comb-over, two bad marriages under his belt, and a chubby paunch hanging over it, on a combination of antidepressants and cheap Scotch flips over the punch bowl? Suddenly, we realize maybe Pinot Noir wasn't so perfect after all. Worse, while we were fawning over Pinot Noir, we missed out on the great wines of Hungary, Dolcetto from Italy, Cava from Spain. How many wines from Alsace and the Loire Valley and Germany and Burgundy did we fail to acquaint ourselves with because we couldn't be bothered to learn their names?

That needs to change.

Then, there is the wine press. I have a great deal of respect for Robert M. Parker Jr. and also for the editors at *Wine Spectator* magazine, but a situation exists in which certain wineries have built them up to a point of reliance. Now, there are virtually no wine brands costing more than $20 a bottle that could survive without marketing dollars and reviews from the wine press. Nearly every single winery relies on the reviews of three critics and deep marketing dollars to build their brands, so the ability of unusual wines—truly innovative wines—to succeed in the market is impaired.

That needs to change.

I've also noticed that the wine world has a bad habit of making otherwise wonderful, decent people act like jerkoffs. You know the type; I refer to them as wine bullies. As I began attending more wine events, I noticed that once people gain a little wine knowledge, they speak down to anyone trying to learn. It became embarrassing to bring friends along to wine tastings because inevitably some hot-shot wine writer or sommelier would pull a spit-take and shout, "What, you actually like that?" You see it in restaurants and homes across America all the time. I mean, you would never walk up to a stranger in a restaurant and say, "I really don't know about those shoes with that skirt, lady," but people seem perfectly comfortable telling a stranger that they think their choice of wine is crap. I've seen people who would never dream of walking into someone's home and announcing the curtains look like something out of the Ropers' *Three's Company* condo but refuse to a drink a wine simply because it's in a 1.5-liter bottle.

That needs to change.

A lot of critics and wine writers are equally guilty of speaking down to the public. People think that because my spit bucket has a New York Jets sticker on it, I'm the guy dumbing down wine, but that's not the case at all. Just because I have a desk full of Thunder-Cats toys does not mean I am not spewing the smartest stuff out there.

That needs to change.

Fortunately, my Web guy, Erik Kastner, introduced me to Web 2.0 and the notion of free content. When Andy Samberg and Chris Parnell's online video *Lazy Sunday* got totally viral in December 2005, I saw the future. I realized I had something to say—something in my chest and in my heart. And that message was not getting out by working eighteen hours a day at Wine Library in New Jersey. So, I sent a stock boy to go buy a video camera, and that was the start of Wine Library TV. Now, I've made the transition from Donald Trump to Mother Teresa, from wine retailer to wine evangelist. With WLTV, I decided to speak to people honestly about wine because it's the best way for me to show my love for people. This book continues that effort.

There is a catch to all this, alluded to in my sign-off. A lot of people really don't like this idea. They don't want the wine world to change. In many ways, the smarter, more confident, and more educated you become, the more dangerous you are to them. They want you to buy wines based strictly on ratings and numbers or their marketing. They want you to blindly follow the critics. They want you to choose wines for their cute labels and catchy commercials and television sponsorships and Hollywood product placements. And they want you to grimace when you taste a wine that smells like Brussels sprouts, or tar, or goat breath, or any flavor that is not within their narrow definition of what wine should be. But I'm telling you to ignore all that—to buy wines that are true to themselves and true to you.

That's how we're going to change the wine world.

How to Taste Wine

Other books promise to teach you everything about wine. I say, go teach yourself. The truth is, I could not teach you the finer points of wine even if I wanted to, because there is only one way to truly understand wine: by tasting it. Reading about wine is like reading about pushups. I can read about pushups all day long. I can read about the perfect form and sets and reps. I can buy nifty gadgets like handgrips for the floor that will tell everyone I'm a pectoral prodigy, a serious pushup kind of guy, but I've accomplished nothing until I get down, palms on the floor, sweat a little, and do a friggin' pushup. There is no other way. Go taste wine.

How do you do that, you ask? A lot of wine books also direct people in the "methodology" of tasting wine. They instruct on serving temperature and glassware, and all those "s's" like swirling and sniffing. I hate that stuff. Tune in to any episode of WLTV and you can watch how I taste wine. I often give my glass a rinse with the wine I'm about to taste. I swirl it and then give it a smell (all right, a little sniffy-sniff), take a swig, and swish it around my mouth.

That's what works for me. But I'm going to assume you already know how to drink out of a glass and how to taste something. In getting started, there is nothing for me to teach you that you did not learn when you left the sippy cup behind and grabbed your first big-boy glass of chocolate milk. Eventually, you'll taste wine in a way that feels natural for you.

Here, then, are my hard-and-fast rules for tasting wine:

1. **Drink wine with people you care about.**
2. **Expand that circle of people at every opportunity.**

That sounds like a lot more fun that sniffing and spitting to me. And in my world, wine is just a vehicle to bring people together.

When wine beginners say they want to learn to taste, they usually mean they want to understand what they are tasting. A lot of people are amazed at how I am able to quickly identify flavors like cotton candy and lead pencil and Skittles in a glass of wine. That comes with time. And like those pushups, it takes diligence and exercise—of your palate. But I'll make a confession to you that I suspect few wine bullies (who in their own minds were born as expert tasters) will ever admit: There was a time when I had serious doubts about my tasting abilities.

I had decided to make wine my life, and the flavors were just not clicking. I started to think it was not going to happen for me, that I might have made a wrong turn. Then, I went to a tasting at the Stage Coach Cafe in Scotch Plains, New Jersey, where I was handed a glass of Masi Amarone, a red wine from northern Italy made with grapes that are dried nearly to the point of becoming raisins. I stuck my nose in the glass and inhaled deeply, as I had so many times before. Suddenly, my nostrils filled with dark chocolate. It was a revelation, as vivid as biting into that Hershey's Dark miniature, the one you never really liked but ate anyway. I was so excited that I had to share the moment; I called my mom. I swear to you, I ran out of the tasting, picked up the phone, and called my mom. Now how am I going to teach you that in a book?

The best way I've found to exercise your palate is to taste everything, and I mean everything—not just wine. Honestly, I probably enjoy a great dinner at Cru or Per Se even more than I enjoy wine because I am truly passionate about food and flavor exploration. There is nothing in this world I won't eat. So, when you see me on WLTV or Conan O'Brien chomping cigars or sucking wet rocks, it's no gimmick. These really are the things that I've done to train my palate. You need to explore every exotic fruit, imported candy, farm stand jam, animal, vegetable, and mineral, because by a miracle of nature, all these flavors can appear in a glass of wine.

101 Wines

I am a man conflicted. It's incredibly ironic that I have chosen to judge products in front of millions of people when I am the most non-judgmental person you could ever hope to meet. I honestly hate tasting wine and having to tell people—nice people—including farmers and winemakers and winery owners, that I think their wine sucks. Lying is just not an option. So, instead I wind up hurting someone's feelings, or even their livelihood. Frankly, just thinking about it makes me sick.

You have no idea how difficult it was for me to select just 101 wines out of the tens of thousands of contenders I tasted. But what I need you to remember is that this is one man's opinion. These are not the greatest wines made this year, but the wines that most excite me. I hope you like these wines; I hope you like what I am doing; I hope you learn something. But please, never put my opinion before your own. There is a whole bunch of people out there that call themselves the Anti-Vayniacs. They buy every wine that I pan and skip the ones I rate highly. They are like Darth Vader—necessary to restore balance to the force. And I love them for that. Some of them have eventually found that they do share my opinion and have left the Anti coalition. But think about how much more they've learned in their wine journey than someone who blindly follows one critic's picks.

These wines are not the 101 best wines. Again, these are the 101 wines that I am most excited about and want to recommend to anyone interested in wine, whether you are a beginner, intermediate, or expert wine lover. These are the "it" wines, the real shizz, the wines that bring the thunder. Of course, quality is paramount, and each wine in this book is truly superb. I also considered value, which is not to be confused with price. A wine that offers value over-delivers for its price: I look for $10 wines that taste more like $30, and also $200 wines that taste like $5,000.

Beyond that, I have selected wines that break down barriers, create new styles, and ooze charisma. Not all of these wines necessarily suit my personal taste, but they all present balance and harmony and thought. Some of them take part in charitable giving or seek to revive grape varieties that have not been made commercially for 10,000 years. I also selected wines that are "double-bubbles," meaning that I enjoy them both alone and with food. In short, these are some damn exciting wines. These are the wines I would recommend to my best friend.

In reconciling my role as a judge and critic, I figure the only way to redeem myself is to truly consider all comers, to give everyone a fair shot. For example, here is a short list of what was *not* left out of the running for my 101 wines: pink wines, sweet wines, wines with funny names, wines with ugly labels, wines costing under $3, wines from terrible vintages, wines with screw caps, wines in magnum bottles, wines in half bottles, wines made from more than just grapes, wines I have hated in the past, wines from people who hate me, wines from people who hate the Jets, and wines whose winemakers have kicked me squarely in the balls. If a wine truly has the chops, it's in the book.

I'll tell you what has been left out: wines you will never find. I ignored thousands of great wines because they did not have widespread distribution or because the current supply would be exhausted by the time this book hit the shelves. The problem with many wine books is that by the time the book is in print, all the wines have disappeared or been replaced by newer vintages. That's about as useful as a 1982 phone directory. At least one wine book has even stopped including vintages altogether. To me, that's insulting. Part of the beauty of making wine is that you get a fresh start every year, and no one can categorically say that a future vintage will taste like the last.

In order to taste future releases for this book, a great number of wineries and distributors collaborated to get me advance bottlings and even barrel samples. For a while there, it seemed like every day a case of wine with handwritten labels was hitting the Newark Airport tarmac and making its way to my tasting table. One importer begged to fly me to Spain for the weekend to taste wines there, while another told me in exasperation that getting these samples was the most difficult assignment he'd ever undertaken. So, I sincerely thank everyone who busted their humps and submitted wines for consideration. Thanks to them, I can truly bring you the wines of 2008. Not all the wines in this book are necessarily out there in large quantities, but with some quick action and a little determination, I think you stand a great chance of locating many of these wines.

In the end, these 101 wines represent the results of a living and breathing contest that I have been conducting every day. A few of them may be wines I have reviewed on an episode of WLTV, or enjoyed on a picnic with a friend. They are simply the most exciting wines I have encountered and now want to share them with you.

Some skeptics will say I'm just out to sell more wine. The truth is, you don't need to taste any of these wines to enjoy the book. If you've read this far and are willing to learn about these wines, I'm sure you've grasped my philosophy: This whole situation is supposed to be fun. If you're able to incorporate that into your own approach to wine, we've both succeeded.

However, if you're a person who really wants to understand wine, and know about wine, there is only one way to do that—by tasting. If you want to learn Chinese history, read; if you wants six-pack abs, do situps; if you want the view from the Eiffel Tower, go there; if you want to know wine, taste. And, taste new wines all the time. I can't emphasize this enough. After all, a fair taste is all that any wine asks of you. Wine doesn't want to be put on pedestal. Wine doesn't want you to change who you are. When you go to a wine tasting, there is no need to take notes, or fake an accent, or talk down to people, or be intimidated, or put on a jacket and tie, or be anything that you're not. So, I hope to see you out tasting wine soon. I'll be the guy in the Jets jersey.

Understanding the

RANKING

The wines are listed in ascending order to the most exciting wine of the year, ranked at number 1.

WINE

Winery name, followed by wine name and vintage year. The vintage represents the vintage that was tasted, which was the current vintage in the market at the time of publication.

PRICE

Prices may vary across markets and with currency fluctuations. The price listed represents the suggested retail price per one 750 ml bottle unless otherwise specified.

ORIGIN

Most wine-producing nations have strict laws governing areas of production, grape varieties, and vinification. In France, the strictest controls are defined under the Appellation d'Origine Contrôlée, or AOC system. The Denominazione di Origine Controllata (DOC) of Italy and Denominación de Origen Calificada (DOCa) of Spain are similar certifications of origin.

#64

THE POWER OF PINK

Wine Information

GRAPES

Not all wines are made entirely from one grape—even if only one is listed on the label. These are the grapes and their percentage in the final blend according to the winery.

ABV

Alcohol by volume.

PRODUCTION

The total number of cases produced or imported to the United States. For standard 750 ml bottles, the figure is based on twelve-bottle cases, although the actual quantity per case may vary.

WINERY WEB SITE

A good source for additional information.

Slowine, Rosé, 2007; $13
Overberg, South Africa
Grapes: Pinot Noir (49%), Pinotage (39%), Shiraz (12%)
12.5% ABV
1,000 cases imported
www.slowine.co.za

A CHÂTEAUNEUF IMPERSONATOR

This wine kicks off my list for totally over-delivering on value. At 44 bones, it may be an expensive wine for the south of France, but what it actually brings is the quality and flavor of top-notch Châteauneuf-du-Pape that would easily fetch $75. It is so similar to Châteauneuf, it's like watching a really great Elvis impersonator—you are so engaged, it feels like watching the real thing. And this guy is good. He starts off rocking the youthful, vibrant, "Blue Suede Shoes" Elvis, then seamlessly transitions to the badass-black-leather-1968-comeback-special Elvis—because this wine can do it all. It is not only delicious, but has something for almost every wine lover.

For the New World fruit bomb fans out there, there is a huge explosion of fruit that is so clean and gorgeous, with seductive strawberry flavors that are incredibly sultry. I'm listening to my glass and instead of "snap, crackle, pop," I hear these lusciously plump berries whispering, "Gary, you know you want me." All that fruit is mixed with this taffy-toffee thing and some sticky cough syrup. But beyond the initial bomb of fruit, there is some pepper, and a little smoky ham and bacon along with this great structure and backbone on the palate that will have Old World fans totally pumped. There is also a little bit of leather strap, like chewing on leather, or standing in the outfield trying to fix the lace on your baseball glove with your teeth. The two are coming together, all intertwined and totally balanced.

Mas de la Barben, Les Calices, 2003; $44
AOC Coteaux du Languedoc, France
Grapes: Grenache (90%), Syrah and Cinsault (10%)
15% ABV
800 cases produced

If you want to get the flavor, I need you to take some pigs-in-a-blanket—you know, those mini hot dogs. Now you're going to take a strawberry Fruit Roll-Up and wrap on one more layer. That's right. We're going one more layer! Now bite it. Eat it. Sprinkle some black pepper on it! That is this wine.

This wine simply rocks—it has a huge mid-palate, and it's kicking this encore through the long finish. It can really handle all your biggest foods, from boar to Châteaubriand. If the dollar were in a good place right now, this wine would be a total steal, because the values coming out of these southern regions of France are just blowing me away. And the way in which these grapes truly resemble one of the great Rhône reds is just uncanny. Ladies and gentlemen, Les Calices has left the building.

Palate Primer:

Fruit Roll-Ups

Based on traditional fruit leather, Fruit Roll-Ups are snacks manufactured by Betty Crocker and distributed by General Mills. According to urban legend, Roll-Ups have their unique parallelogram shape because their design and production were inspired by the coiled cardboard of a toilet paper tube. Flavors include Electric Blue Raspberry, Flavor Wave, Strawberry, and Strawberry Kiwi Kick.

MAKING MOM PROUD

#100

ome qualities about this wine border on what I'm against, but it also does a lot of things that I'm totally for. First of all, it represents a great project, and I am totally proud to support brothers Erik and Alex Bartholomaus who lost their mother, Liliana, to breast cancer. Fifty cents from the sale of each bottle of this wine goes to breast cancer research. That's a pretty nice chunk of the $13 admission price, and the results are approaching a million dollars.

The 2 Brothers Cab also represents something great for all the people just getting started on value-priced Cabernet. This wine is a little artificial for me at times, but I also believe it holds a lot of the same appeal of wines like Yellow Tail: It's just plain old-fashioned tasty. So I want those of you drinking $10 Cab to think of this as Yellow Tail 2.0. Make the upgrade and feel good about it!

On the nose—okay, I'm not going to sugarcoat this—I smell some stink bomb. I'm expecting to hear my fourth-grade teacher start screaming because this clearly has that sulphury chemical stink bomb smell. But underneath that stink lurks this beef jerky component, which brings it back to smelling

Label Lore

The 2 Brothers labels are designed by brother Alex Bartholomaus, a renowned tattoo artist, with their mother's favorite symbol, the fleur-de-lis. The new Reserva line also includes a Syrah and a German Riesling.

2 Brothers, Cabernet Sauvignon Reserva, 2005; $13
Colchagua Valley, Chile
Grape: Cabernet Sauvignon
13.9% ABV
6,000 cases imported
www.bigtattooed.com

really tasty, along with some beautiful blackberry aromas. You have to take that wineglass and just roll it and roll it in your hand until you have carpal tunnel to release the fruit.

On the palate—hello SweeTarts! Actually, there is a whole circa-1950s five-and-dime candy rack, with all these cherry and grape Bottle Caps candies and gobs of blueberry jam. The fruit is very candied, very soft. It's like that Hostess blueberry pie, where the blueberry is obviously chemically engineered, but you can't help loving it anyway. That's where I am with this wine. So, I know this might be a little New World for some other people as well, but give it a chance. There is some licorice in there—not the really good black licorice you get in France, but the junky stuff we have here in America. But hey, I love that too.

So yes, this is a little candied, a little fake. And yes, I'm a big softy for charity. But this is also a truly tasty entry-level red wine that is far more real than a lot of other stuff you're probably drinking at this price.

WINES OF EMPOWERMENT

The former apartheid government of South Africa has a lot to be ashamed of, but the current wine industry is taking some positive steps, especially with these aptly named Fairvalley wines. The infamous "dop system," in which farm workers were paid a portion of their wages in wine, was a colonial institution, aimed at encouraging alcoholism and servitude. While it was outlawed in the 1960s, reports in *US News & World Report* as recently as 2002 claimed the system was still evident, and the pernicious social effects clearly continue.

That's why the Fairvalley Workers Association, founded in 1997 with funding from the South African government and winemaker Charles Back (owner of Fairview Winery and creator of the famed Goats do Roam), is such a huge step for the entire South African wine industry. Rather than labor for someone else, Fairvalley winemaker Awie Adolf has a cellar to call his own on the 38-acre farm adjacent to Fairview. As the farm continues to grow, vineyards and homes are being established there.

Right off the bat, what I love is that this wine really represents Pinotage. This wine has a distinct banana peel on the nose, which is really fun to recognize. It also has some bacon fat, almost like I forgot the bacon on the stove.

This wine is fairly light, not the most complex wine in the world. It's not a show-stopping wine, but at $10 it's a young, fun, everyday

Fairvalley, Pinotage, 2006; $10
South Africa
Grape: Pinotage
14.7% ABV
3,300 cases produced
www.capewine.com

Meet the Grape: Pinotage

Pinotage is a cross between Pinot Noir and Cinsault grapes, developed in South Africa by Professor Abraham Izak Perold in 1925. It is still almost exclusively grown in South Africa. Although Syrah is the primary grape of Hermitage in the Rhône Valley, Cinsault goes by the name Hermitage in South Africa, resulting in the moniker "Pinotage."

wine that I think many people can and will enjoy. It has sweet tannins, great freshness, and a bittersweet balance of cassis that I think will seduce a lot of people. With its nice long finish and dry tannins, this is a great wine to pair with pizza or spaghetti. And I think the rustic character gives it the potential to really bring some thunder. This is Fairvalley's sixth vintage of Pinotage, and I think we have great things to look forward to from them. I really enjoy this wine, both what it does for me as a wine lover and what it does for an African community.

MORE THAN
I BARGAINED FOR

Every wine lover needs a school-night red. That's a wine that costs under 10 bucks and is perfect with soccer-mom standbys like pizza and pasta—a pop, pour, and drink wine. Jumilla, an up-and-comer among the Spanish quality wine regions, is proving to be a great place to find these wines.

This particular red includes a pretty eclectic blend of grapes. There is even a little touch of Petit Verdot, and you know I am down with the PV. Now, usually I expect a school-night wine to come at me with a lot of fruit; for the money, I can't demand much more than that. That's precisely why the incredible charcoal, leather, and venison aromas on this wine are such an exciting bonus. This is very Rhône-like, aromatically interesting right from the start, more like something you'd expect to smell on a $30 to $40 Châteauneuf-du-Pape. One contributor is the Monastrell, which is not only the predominant grape variety in Jumilla, making up about 85 percent of the vines, but also goes by the name Mourvèdre in the Rhône Valley.

Overall, this wine is extremely gamy. I feel like I'm a hunter and I just killed a wild boar and ripped it open and took a bite. But before I did, I think I spread strawberry jam all over it. Man, that was a strange thing to do, but it really worked. These classic flavors of wild gaminess, leather, and strawberry jam are very much something I'd expect to find in the Languedoc, the Rhône, and now—apparently— Jumilla. The variety of flavors in here is simply enormous, with

Caracol Serrano, Tinto Joven, 2005; $9

DO Jumilla, Spain

Grapes: Monastrell (50%), Syrah (30%), Cabernet Sauvignon (19%), Merlot and Petite Verdot (less than 1%)

14% ABV

12,000 cases imported

wine country

The DO Jumilla is planted squarely in the southeast quarter of Spain. Vine-killing Phylloxera arrived in Jumilla in 1989, about 100 years *after* it devastated most of Europe, providing a need for vineyard replanting and contributing to the recent revitalization.

secondary peppery pomegranate flavors on the finish. This wine is clearly far more complex than its price point, and it's always exciting when a wine tastes like way more than it costs.

Not only does this wine fulfill my pizza and pasta requirement, but you have my permission to pour on the Bolognese or sear off a steak. You should also consider brown-bagging this wine for your wine geek friends, because once you see the label, it's very hard to believe the earthy, rustic, gamy complexity of this wine. What you really need to do is plan a tasting where everyone has to bring a wine up to $30 in a paper bag, and throw this red into the mix. Not only will it probably clean up, but I guarantee everyone will be buying a case the next day. This everyday value will please serious red wine drinkers and represents the kind of wine that I want to be drinking next Wednesday night. After tasting it, you'll understand why.

P.S. I LOVE YOU

My first sniffy-sniff of this wine immediately reminded me of some fertilizer they put down with the sod in my development in Edison, New Jersey. (Big shout-out to Dogwood Meadows 1985!) This aroma is really exotic, and in some ways really personal, but I'm never afraid to say what I smell in a wine and nor should you be. The fertilizer is coupled with these big, dark blackberries. You know the ones that are so sweet and so ripe, they just fall apart in your hands and you think the stain will never come off? *Those* berries! Finally, there is a melted vanilla ice cream. There is a little oak monster (*aaaaaaahhhh!*) making a cameo in here, but he's wearing camouflage, like Corporal Kirschner, WWF-circa-1985 style.

I'm not surprised at the intrigue of this wine, because Petite Sirah is responsible for some of the most interesting, complex, and monstrous wines in America at the moment. There are a lot of zealous PS fans out there. Perhaps more than anything else, Petite Sirah is known for its color. And true to form, this wine is so inky, so black, that I feel like an octopus got really pissed off at me and I captured his anger in this glass.

Sometimes you can almost describe wine by color, and I feel like this wine would actually be a very complex mix of brown, purple, and black. That's one you won't find on the color wheel. It is all these dark colors, because in addition to blackberries, it is so tannic that this

Nord Estate Wines, Petite Sirah Jonquil Vineyards, 2004; $40
Napa Valley, California
14.9% ABV
Grapes: Petit Sirah (95%), Merlot (5%)
194 cases produced
www.napavalleyvineyard.com

wine is getting medieval on you. The obvious cocoa flavors of Count Chocula are in there, too. Overall, this wine is very well balanced with good structure and loads of fruit just finding its way into every corner of my mouth. It is so dry my mouth is puckered up like Granny's chin.

I find this to be a fascinating example of PS, and it is truly up my alley. I am desperate to pair this wine with food, but the only thing I can think of to possibly pair with it is wild boar, the kind I used to hunt with my Rambo knife back in my development in Edison, New Jersey.

Meet the Grape:
Petite Sirah

Also known as Durif in France, Petite Sirah has a long history as a blending grape, valued for adding color and tannin to red blends. Although an offspring of Peloursin and Syrah, Petite Sirah bears little resemblance to its namesake and parent Syrah.

A WHITE FOR
THE RED LOVERS

Too many people get a little bit of wine knowledge under their belt and suddenly feel like they need to start dissing white wine. So, here is a white wine that I think could totally bring those hard-core red wine drinkers back to reality. If you only like red wine with your steak, I challenge you to pop this with your filet mignon or other rich foods. You may realize just how serious white wine can be.

This white, made from 100 percent Viognier, shows the grape's classic oiliness, like extra-virgin olive oil meets espresso and lemon peel, along with a coiled-up garden hose. It is very garage-oriented yet aromatically very pretty, with apricots and peaches in there. This is a big red wine lover's nose on a white wine.

The flavor is filled with beautiful peach-mango coming through on the mid-palate, and the gorgeous acidity really envelops the palate, followed by a very nice dryness. A pure Viognier with this kind of acidity and vibrancy is actually quite rare, because this grape's massive body and richness often seem to dominate the balance. It is very Rhône-like in its approach, with the complexity of many of the classic Marsanne, Roussanne, and Viognier blends. Some big lime flavors are also bouncing around in there. This is very ripe, very serious stuff, and, to be honest, probably not really appealing for your typical white wine drinker. I would not be surprised if only 10 percent of people reading actually appreciate this wine, with its serious approach and great polish. And it sells for close to $50, so we're well into the big red

Ascheri, Montalupa Bianco Viognier, 2004; $48
VdT, Piedmont, Italy
Grape: Viognier
13.5% ABV
400 cases produced
www.ascherivini.it

Meet the Grape:
Viognier

As recently as the 1960s, Viognier was growing almost exclusively in its home appellations of Condrieu and Château-Grillet in the Northern Rhône. Small amounts are also traditionally blended into the powerful Syrahs of Côte-Rôtie. However, with more recent plantings, full-bodied, highly aromatic white wines are now produced from Viognier in California, Washington, Australia, and even Italy.

league pricewise, too. This wine is just so very complex, with hints of bluestone, rocks, and minerals, and an almost escargot shell sensation, all layered together with ripe gourmet-grocery apricots. We all go through phases in our wine drinking, and I think many of us have been in that teenage know-it-all stage where we start ripping on how lame everything is. Once we've come to really appreciate red wine, we don't want to be seen hanging out with white wines, or sweet wines, or pink wines. But the wisest drinker is the one who will visit the same wines again and again, with a smarter palate each time.

So, all you serious, devout red wine drinkers, I think you are exactly the people who will understand why this wine is different, special, and complex. C'mon. Quit hating on the white.

#95

NOT YOUR FATHER'S SPUMANTE

Please, don't let the name Spumante fool you. Italian sparkling wines get really beaten up because people think they are strictly Moscato d'Asti, Prosecco, and Asti Spumante. In general, many people believe all Italian sparkling wines are sweet, or at least inferior to those of Champagne and even California. But after tasting this wine, I'm ready to smash those preconceptions.

First off, the word *spumante* has nothing to do with sweetness, or even flavor. It literally means "foaming" and is a measure of the amount of fizz in the bottle. And, if you know your grapes, you'll see this wine is made from both white (Fiano) and red (Aglianico) varieties, similar to many Champagnes.

On the nose, I get starfruit, which I really love. It's an exceptional fruit and one you detect in a lot of white grapes, so you want to get familiar with the flavor. There is also a very specific Argentine honey that I like, and I can envision it being poured all over the starfruit, which is so perplexing and fresh. On the tail end of the nose, it has an almost honeycomb aroma. On the palate,

Label Lore

The de Conciliis family are jazz music aficionados. Their red wine, Naima, takes its name from a John Coltrane song, written for his first wife of the same name. This wine is actually named for Miles Davis; Selim is an anagram of his name.

there are these little pears that you can find in the gourmet stores, and they are so fresh and delicious.

There are many, many sparkling wines from France and the U.S. that cost $30 to $40 and fail to offer this type of complexity and focus. This fruit is dialed in like a sniper rifle on your palate. There is a touch of sugarcane quality that you won't find in many brut wines, but I would not say that this wine is anywhere close to sweet. The fruit is just so fresh, so explosive, so ripe that it beams through. It is getting harder and harder to find reasonably priced, quality sparklers, so to find this wine for under $20 makes me really optimistic that I'll be popping bubbles for a very long time.

Palate Primer:

Starfruit

When cut across its ridges, starfruit, also known as carambola, reveals a five-pointed star. The fruit is crunchy, with a balance of sweetness and acidity, and may have flavors of pears, apples, or grapes. Originally native to Sri Lanka and Indonesia, starfruit is readily available in specialty grocery stores in the U.S.

STICKY NAVELS ALL AROUND

It's very difficult as a wine critic to review dessert wines because they are just so delicious. These wines have the unfair advantage of all that sugar that reels you in and seduces you. However, I've tasted at least fifteen dessert wines for this book and am limiting myself to just a few. This one makes my short list.

Picolit is one of the great Italian dessert wines—one of the world's great dessert wines, for that matter—and this has an aroma that has me just dying to get into it. Talk about honeysuckle and peaches and apricot: This has it all. In fact, it smells exactly like honey-covered tangerines. I also get a little butterscotch, a little caramel. It's almost Sauternes-like to the point that I just found my mouth watering for foie gras. Now, that is one weird Pavlovian response that tells you a little about how my brain is wired.

The orange-tangerine component of this is just beautiful. And while it's a little bit of a splurge, it will not seem so expensive when I tell you that without a doubt this Picolit rivals any of the best six Puttonyos Hungarian Tokay as well as any top $100 to $200 Sauternes from Château d'Yquem, Château Suduiraut, and Château Climens. It has the big acidic backbone of Sauternes coupled with the over-the-top deliciousness of Tokay, along with an interesting banana peel flavor on the finish that just amazes me.

I hate to get too wine-nerdy on you, but Friuli is a great place for white wines in general, and here is this inspiring caramel-tangerine-

Rocca Bernarda, Picolit, 2005; $85/500 ml
DOC Colli Orientali del Friuli, Italy
Grape: Picolit
13% ABV
200 cases produced
www.roccabernarda.com

orange dessert wine, with so much elegance and passion, and so few people have ever tried it. This is so overlooked and so sensual, I need to get a little X-rated with my imagery. This wine makes you want to put on the Barry White and lap it off someone's belly. It's more like you and your teenage dream date are ending a summer night sharing an ice cream sundae at the Jersey shore. You are feeding eat other as it melts, and this sundae has not only peaches-and-cream ice cream, but bananas, warm caramel, and butterscotch sauce. Your lips are all sticky with it, and the second you finish the last spoonful, you lean in and land your first kiss. It is *that* good, and *that* gorgeous, and *that* memorable, and you need to find it.

Meet the Grape: Picolit

Grown almost exclusively in the northern Italian region of Friuli, Picolit is a rare and low-yielding grape variety that takes its name from the Italian word *piccolo*, or "small." It is used to make both dry and sweet wines, the latter often produced by drying the grapes for even greater concentration.

#93 BURGUNDY WITH BUBBLES

Champagne is becoming more and more out of reach for everyday consumers, with even basic bottles topping 40 bones. So what's a guy who loves the crackle of sparkling wine (and Pop Rocks) to do? Personally, I am on a Zelda-like quest for great deals in sparkling wines from places *outside* Champagne. And even though I consider myself a tough critic of sparklers, this Blanc de Blanc from Burgundy just bowled me over.

Blanc de Blanc, as in Champagne, designates that the wine is made entirely from white grapes. Unlike Champagne, however, there are a number of white grapes in Burgundy, and this wine includes two of them—Chardonnay and Aligoté—resulting in a nose that offers a beautiful rum-raisin component with a glimpse of apple fruit, along with fresh-baked bread, including all that beautiful yeastiness that I really adore.

The flavor is clean and crisp, with beautiful elegance. For sparkling wine, this comes incredibly close to real Champagne, with an awesome Cinnamon Toast Crunch

Label Lore

"Crémant" is commonly used to identify sparkling wines from regions other than Champagne in France. Many regions that produce still wines also produce crémant from the same grapes, including wines like Crémant d'Alsace, Crémant de Bourgogne, Crémant de Limoux, Crémant de Loire, and even Crémant de Bordeaux.

Didier Montchovet, Crémant de Bourgogne, Blanc de Blanc, 2004; $27
AOC Crémant de Bourgogne, France
Grapes: Chardonnay (80%), Aligoté (20%)
12% ABV
50 cases imported
www.montchovet.fr

component on the mid-palate, and this beautiful acidity that is very, very long. This is a throwback to fifteen years ago, when you could find Champagne with great complexity priced in the 20s; that is unheard of in Champagne today! I know you're addicted to the Clicquot "yellow label," but I want you to put it down, step outside the box, and grab this beautiful gold-labeled crémant. This producer has done a really amazing job, and it is almost like going back in time, to an era when great French bubbly was accessible and fairly priced. With this wine priced under $30, it's right in the sweet spot—pop it for Sunday brunch, a dinner party, or even New Year's.

Meet the Grape: Aligoté

Considered the "other white grape" of Burgundy, Aligoté does not generally enjoy the prestige of Chardonnay and is known for producing simple, thin, high-acid wines. The grape is primarily used in sparkling wines and in the still AOC wines Bourgogne Aligoté and Bouzeron Aligoté. It is also planted in Bulgaria, Romania, and Switzerland.

LAST OF THE BUDGET BORDEAUX

I n 1989, a new baseball card company called Upper Deck entered the market. They were making high-end cards with full-color pictures on the *backs*, using holograms and UV protection. They combined high quality with high demand and a deliberate shortage of cards, and the price of a pack of baseball cards changed forever. (There is a point to this. Stick with me.)

In 2005, there was a similar perfect storm in Bordeaux. Quality— and prices—for Bordeaux wines went through the roof. Now, the dollar is practically Monopoly money in Europe, and the thought process, pricing, and branding of Bordeaux wine have taken a monumental turn—one that I don't see reversing. Therefore, if you are reading this, I really encourage you to find any and all of the 2004 Bordeaux on my list. There is very strong rationale that you may never have a chance to taste wines like this at these prices again. (Bonus tip: You may also want to add to that shopping list 2001, a comparable vintage that is still sitting on some shelves.)

On the nose of this wine, you cannot escape the smoky barbecue aroma. We've got Southern hospitality in the house, and I think they

VAYNERCABULARY

Barbecue-esque (adj)—*while the term is used interchangeably with grilling in some parts of the U.S., true barbecue is slowly smoked over smoldering wood at low temperatures. These flavors are often apparent in oak-aged red wines.*

Château Beaumont Haut-Médoc, 2004; $20
AOC Cru Bourgeois Supérieur, Haut-Médoc, France
Grapes: Merlot (48%), Cabernet Sauvignon (46%),
  Cabernet Franc (4%), Petit Verdot (2%)
13% ABV
5,000 cases imported
www.chateau-beaumont.com
www.bobbofman.com

are smoking Porky Pig's snout in an iron skillet. This is very barbecue-esque, very smoky. I also get some really interesting cassis and goji berries. I like to assign personality traits to wine, and this wine is very clever. It throws a smoke bomb at you, and as it dissipates, it reveals all these underlying flavors.

The first nanosecond of this wine is pure bitterness, as the tannins attack. But it immediately turns S^2—silky and smooth—and that will win me over every time. The smoky, dusty component is in charge here, with the dark, black cocoa blocking out the yellow raspberry fruit. However, I think that fruit is going to emerge over the next year or so. If you want to drink this now, I need to issue a two-hour decant alert. Two hours of aeration is guaranteed to get some of the hidden fruit to come out to play. So get out there and find this steal of a 2004 Bordeaux and other wines like it now. It's certainly not going to get any easier.

OPPORTUNITY KNOCKS

When good fortune delivers an amazing vintage like Bordeaux 2005, you don't need to drop $700 a bottle to enjoy it. Few of us are wine collectors, and, frankly, the bragging rights that come with these pricey wines excite me a whole lot less than this basic $13 Bordeaux with huge QPR. This is the essence of a great vintage; quality is everywhere.

This wine is mainly Merlot-based, and, according to the producer, the property used to be part of Saint-Émilion, which makes sense to me because it reminds me of those wines, but at a much better price. This wine shows great backbone and a nice charcoal, Canadian bacon component. It is almost like a diner breakfast, because along with that bacon, the mid-palate reveals a smattering of pancake batter. It has this oak and vanilla that is reminiscent of pancakes—and I am loving it. This wine is very rich and heavy on the palate, with an impressive spectrum of flavors, including a finish of green bell peppers and Brussels sprouts.

Palate Primer:

Brussels Sprouts

As part of the family of vegetables including cabbage, collard greens, broccoli, and kale, Brussels sprouts resemble small cabbages in appearance and flavor. The vegetable takes its name from its Belgian city of origin, although it has been cultivated in some form since Roman times.

Château de la Cour d'Argent, 2005; $13
AOC Côtes de Castillon, Bordeaux, France
Grapes: Merlot (95%), Cabernet Franc and Cabernet Sauvignon (5%)
12.5% ABV
10,000 cases produced
www.denis-barraud.com
www.bobbofman.com

This wine really reminds me of many $20 Bordeaux I've been drinking from other vintages. It offers an impressively heavy $20 or $30 mouthfeel. Looking at many recent solid—but not stellar—vintages like 1999, 2001, and 2003, you would have to climb much higher up the ladder to find this kind of quality. If you want to experience Bordeaux without spending a lot of money, I promise this wine will deliver everything you want, and it is drinking tremendously right now. While your wine bully buddies are waiting for their trophy wines to mature in the cellar, you can be drinking bottle after bottle of these delicious basic Bordeaux and still have enough money left to get the premium cable package and maybe even a few pay-per-views. These are the wines that make 2005 so very special.

wine country

Côtes de Castillon is regarded as a region of escalating quality, producing Merlot-based wines that draw frequent comparison to the wines of Saint-Émilion and Pomerol. Historically, the region is also known as the place where the English lost control of Bordeaux, with the defeat of General Talbot in 1453.

#90 THE OTHER RED WINE

wine country

Located 100 miles east of San Francisco, wine grapes have been cultivated in Lodi since the 1850s, and the region was recognized as an AVA in 1986. Today, Lodi has more than 75,000 acres of vineyards farmed by more than 750 growers. With a production that exceeds the amount of grapes in Napa and Sonoma combined, Lodi was long dominated by large wineries, but more boutique wineries are opening there now. www.lodiwine.com

Because most Americans select, buy, and drink their wine by grape variety, it can be tough for a blended wine to gain any respect. More blended wines have been making inroads lately, but far too many people are still hooked on big brands and single varietal wines that simply don't deliver on their cost. Why not try something else, something "Other"?

Even beyond the label with its knock-off Matisse drawing of a naked girl flaunting her butt (which miraculously got the stamp of approval from our TTB bureaucrats), there is a lot to like about this wine. It has dark color, dark chocolate, and dark raspberries on the nose. It is a little bit Batman—just dark, dark, dark! I really like these dark flavors and jammy fruit aromas that are so typical of what's happening in Lodi right now. The wines produced in this region are not the most structured or thought-provoking, but they are some of the more fruit-driven, easy-drinking, good-value wines coming out

Peirano Estate Vineyards, The Other, 2006; $13
Lodi, California
Grapes: Cabernet Sauvignon (60%), Merlot (30%), Syrah (10%)
13.8% ABV
10,000 cases produced
www.peirano.com

of California at the moment. Lodi is the new frontier, much like Paso Robles was ten years ago.

The flavor offers strawberry and a lot of exotic dark fruit, great tannins, and good backbone with nice richness. There is also a secondary flavor of eggplant, which really reminds me of a classic Italian meal. That character, along with all the cherries and strawberries, has cinched my opinion that while this wine may not have a grape name listed on the front label, it is way superior to most of the generic Cab and Merlot I see people drinking in this price range. Whatever you want to call them—blends, mixed grapes, multicultural—these wines are people too.

So please, put down the K-J, the Simi, the Franciscan, the Rodney Strong. Put down the Benzinger, and for God's sake put down the Clos du Bois! Get over the grape variety hang-up. With really pretty fruit and earthy jamminess, this blend of three great grapes offers way more character than many of those one-dimensional wines at the same price.

BUBBLY BARGAIN

I predict that the next few years are going to be tough times for Champagne lovers like me. First, true Champagne comes only from France, and the euro is totally kicking us in the nads because of dollar deterioration. To add to the problem, I think the 2005 Bordeaux and 2005 Burgundy prices are going to trickle over to Champagne, and in the next five years we will see dramatic, radical, and appalling price increases in Champagne.

This concerns me because you know that when I'm forced to name my stranded on a desert island wine, it is bubbly all the way. So, I am totally excited to find these great bubblies from California that represent a value over true Champagne. I think for a long time California did not take bubblies really seriously. It was a marketing opportunity, a commodity, but this effort has me convinced that J is aiming for first-class sparkling wine. This wine is made from all the classic Champagne grape varieties, and J is getting into the rosé and vintage sparkling game, which shows me they are serious about the category.

But nothing better demonstrates their intent than this wine itself,

VAYNERCABULARY

Cuvée (n)—the result of blending wines from several types or sources. In Champagne, the term is commonly used for wines blended from several vintages and vineyards in order to achieve a uniform product year after year.

J Vineyards & Winery, Cuvée 20, N/V; $30

Russian River Valley, California

Grapes: Chardonnay (55%), Pinot Noir (43%),
   Pinot Meunier (2%)

12.5% ABV

17,400 cases produced

www.jwine.com

with an aroma of walnuts, Swee-Tarts, and a little Cinnamon Toast Crunch that I find delicious. In the flavor, there is some amazing Granny Smith apple bouncing around with Sour Patch Kids candy. This is so beautiful and clean it just relaxes me, like a deep massage—not like a Lars-breaking-my-bones massage, but a Sandy-caressing-me massage.

wine country

With a name that honors its original settlers, the Russian River Valley AVA of California benefits from a cool ocean fog that drops evening temperatures as much as 40°F from the daytime high. The cool valley suits many grapes, but is especially renowned for Chardonnay and Pinot Noir.

When I first tasted this non-vintage California bubbly earlier in 2007, I had very low expectations. Thankfully, I was completely wrong. This is extremely well made, and for someone addicted to bubbles like me, it represents a great way to stave off the rising prices of the Clicquots and Moëts of the world. I totally embrace this Champagne—I mean "sparkling wine"—and I think other bubbly fans will too.

THE TRUE COLOR OF PINOT

wine country

Staete Landt was the first European name given to New Zealand by Dutch explorer Abel Tasman in 1642. Modern-day New Zealand includes ten important wine-producing regions, including Marlborough, Gisborne, and Central Otago, which boasts the world's most southerly Chardonnay grapes. www.nzwine.com

It's really incredible what's happened to Pinot Noir since the movie *Sideways*. A lot of winemakers have taken to pumping up their Pinot with a shot of Petit Sirah, an inky-black grape that makes this light red appear much darker—more appealing to macho red wine lovers. It's as if Pinot Noir is secretly trying to become Syrah, or even Cabernet. This wine, however, is pure Pinot—light red in color and just plain pretty. It's great to see a Pinot Noir that isn't ashamed to be itself.

I still think Central Otago is *the* area for Pinot Noir in New Zealand, but this wine proves that Marlborough may also have huge potential. It's a great wine from a single vineyard of just 17 acres.

On the nose, this wine has subtle peppered strawberry aromas. Next comes the smell of a huge red rubber band, like the one you could shoot clear across the classroom. It's almost the smell of the pink rubber bouncer ball that you could rocket over the rooftop on a good bounce, something a little bit plasticesque. But, what I really love about this wine is the tremendous polish—not just the polish that I feel on my palate—I literally get a whiff of walking through

Staete Landt Vineyards, Marlborough Pinot Noir, 2006; $34

Marlborough, New Zealand
Grape: Pinot Noir
14% ABV
800 cases imported
www.staetelandt.co.nz

Grand Central Terminal, bustling past the guys perched in their chairs, getting a shine while waiting for their train. From the first sip, there are a lot of strawberry flavors and also really pretty herbal nuances to this Pinot, with a tea-esque component. The tannins are good and firm for a Pinot. They show clear-cut backbone and that makes me believe this wine will be at its best four to seven years from now. Interestingly, something about this wine just makes me want to eat pig snout! Seriously.

This is clearly a New World Pinot, but I have to love it for being true to its roots. The overall explosion of fruit, sheer vibrancy, and youthfulness lean toward Oregon even more than California. There is clearly a little too much of a sweet fruit, yum-yum factor to be considered Old World. However, the genuine elegance and Burgundian quality to the mouthfeel make this a truly exceptional wine in a world of Pinot pretenders.

SOMETIMES BIGGER IS BETTER

 # 87

The name of this wine leaves no doubt about their position in the Spanish wine industry: This large conglomerate is the numero uno—the largest still wine producer in Spain. We are talking Hillary Clinton confidence with Gallo-size cojones on this wine.

Spain excels in many areas of winemaking these days, and there

wine country

Vino de la Tierra, or country wine, is similar to the French Vin de Pays. Vino de la Tierra comes from a specific region of Spain and shows that region's local characteristics. There are more than forty regions making Vino de la Tierra, but the two most prominent are Vino de la Tierra de Castilla and Vino de la Tierra de Castilla y León.
www.winesfromspain.com

are more than a few premium offerings on this list. But they are also among the few places able to produce solid wines in the $5 to $10 range, and this inexpensive, large-production wine is a great example.

On the nose, this has a charred—very charcoal—component, mixed with blueberry jam and hints of smoke. It's very interesting and clear-cut with its flavors. A lot of Spanish and Australian wines that play around at this price point are very fake, basically Hi-C punch fruit bombs, but this wine is actually very classic in its approach and tastes much more real. It is bright, well made, and polished, with real flavors.

This is not a wine that is going to make you scream with delight or

Bodegas Berberana S.A., Berberano Numero Uno, Tempranillo, 2005; $9

Vino de la Tierra de Castilla, Spain
Grape: Tempranillo
13.5% ABV
13,500 cases imported
www.berberana.com

totally rip your face off. However, it's a wine that is authentic and food-friendly, at a price that you can feel good about on a school night. The tannins in here are actually really nice, so this wine will last about as long as an open Twinkie, three to four years.

As far as food, we're talking Wednesday night dinner. Pair this with chicken wings, pizza, Italian subs, or an In-N-Out burger. There are times when I like to contrast my wine with my meal: have Chinese and Champagne, or burgers with cult-Cab—just to dress up an otherwise ordinary dinner. And then there are the nights when you realize a slice of pizza is now $2.50 in New York, and you're gonna need a red wine that can compete with a two-liter Coke for value. It's not fast food; it's commodity food. And this red from a behemoth of Spain is an example of a great commodity wine.

Palate Primer

Hi-C

Launched in 1948 by Niles Foster, Hi-C was originally an orange-flavored drink and takes its name from the inclusion of vitamin C. Today, Hi-C is one of the largest-selling products of the Coca-Cola Company, and the many flavors contain only 10 percent fruit juice, but 100 percent of the US RDA of vitamin C per serving.

OAK MONSTER BE DAMNED

I think Chardonnay, more than any other wine, got totally out of control with its oak monster. Far too often, the oak monster comes in, smashes all the fruit flavors and freshness, and leaves this wine tasting like a splintered two-by-four. So, I'm really passionate about this whole movement for *unoaked* Chardonnay. I tasted dozens of them searching for an example for this list before this one totally grabbed me.

You see, the problem with a lot of unoaked Chardonnay is that they try to be Sauvignon Blanc. That comes off like a last-minute Halloween costume. It's like they don't want to be oaky Chardonnay, so they go into their dad's closet, grab his old suit jacket, and put together some lame costume instead of being something truly original.

You should never be scared to articulate what you smell in a wine, and to me this smells like Prosecco. (Yes, I know Prosecco is another wine, but who says one wine can't smell like another?) It's actually like Prosecco and apples mixed together. If you love green apples, you need to go buy this wine now! Although this is a still white wine, it really gives me the aroma of a crisp sparkling wine.

Another thing many unoaked Chardonnays lack is serious weight, but this Chard has it big-time. It has a honeyesque quality, nice acidity, and great balance, along with an extremely long finish, which is one of the biggest things I look for in a wine. You should have some

Gunn Estate, Unoaked Chardonnay, 2007; $16
New Zealand
Grape: Chardonnay
13% ABV
750 cases imported
www.gunnestate.co.nz

time to taste the wine. I mean, you paid for it; you drank it. If you're not going to taste it for more than a split second, drink tap water and save yourself a crapload of money. As the finish rolls on, I am tasting not just green apple, but almost a dried apricot flavor with a spritz of lemon. I am *really* feeling this wine, and I think it will continue to flesh out and have even more weight by the time you're drinking it. This is great Chardonnay, pure and simple. Screw the oak monster.

Meet the Grape:
Chardonnay

Chardonnay is one of the few white grapes that benefits from oak. Even in Burgundy and Champagne, where it is the premier white grape, Chardonnay typically undergoes some oak aging. Unoaked Chardonnay is a reaction to the extreme "oak monster" unleashed by many New World winemakers.

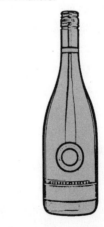

JEKYLL AND HYDE

Throughout this book, you'll hear me describe wine as New World—ripe, bold, fruit-driven—and Old World—nuanced, classic, subdued. Of course these are generalizations, but occasionally a wine has the best of both "worlds."

This Hungarian Chardonnay has pleasant oak and butter aromas on the nose, but they are very Burgundian in style, much more subtle than most of their California counterparts. There is also a really interesting clove coming through. It reminds me of biting on a clove, which I did once on Wine Library TV. Cloves are one thing that I actually recommend you don't put in your mouth—not unless you have a toothache, because it numbed my entire mouth. Apparently, some dentists still use clove gel in place of Novocain. Who knew?

In the flavor, the Old World style keeps coming, with this lively, very Chablis-like acidity, flavors of bluestone, and what I like to call crab claws—like these crabs that just came out of the sea and are all salty and stony and fresh. Then, just when I think I have it figured

---

VAYNERCABULARY

Hyde vineyards (n)—one of the most famous California vineyards, started by Larry Hyde in 1979 in the region that would become the Carneros AVA. The 150-acre estate is planted with seven types of Chardonnay and other grape varieties and contributes grapes for the production of ten vineyards' wines from producers including HdV, Kistler Vineyards, Robert Mondavi, Merryvale, Paul Hobbs, and Patz and Hall.

Monarchia Winery, Battonage Chardonnay, 2006; $20
Eger, Hungary
Grape: Chardonnay
14.2% ABV
850 cases produced
www.monarchiawinery.com

out, this wine does a total Jekyll and Hyde, literally like a Hyde vineyard from California, unleashing all its creaminess and butter and weight. And I am *loving* it!

I really like that this Chardonnay hits both ends of the spectrum, which is not an easy thing to do. It's clean and clever. The flavors are really focused, with great gooseberry and butterscotch flavors in the mid-palate that linger through the finish. This wine just engages me and curtails my entire palate. That is where it really succeeds, in completely covering my entire palate, and I respect and appreciate that. The change-up has me really excited, and instead of Old World crispness, there is this long finish; this lushness, richness, and complexity. This wine is a huge home run and a Chardonnay that a lot of people will respond to and enjoy, regardless of which world they prefer.

Label Lore

Although you're more likely to see it on the back label of a wine than the front, in this case, Monarchia boasts of its *battonage*. Following fermentation, dead yeast cells sinks to the bottom of the fermenter or barrel. Many winemakers choose to age the wine *sur lie* or "on top of the yeast," or lees, to impart bready, biscuity, and nutty flavors, especially in the case of Chardonnay. Stirring the lees to heighten and integrate those flavors even more is a process known as *battonage*.

TEROLDEGO WINS BY A NOSE

It's great to see an Italian grape do something exciting in California. This is probably going to offend some people, but for the most part, Sangiovese in California has failed. Dolcetto has failed, and so has Barbera. I expected so much from these grapes, but they have been unable to conquer the California climate and even come close to what they do in Italy. Who would have ever thought Teroldego might be the grape to make it happen? Yet this is one of the finer examples of an Italian varietal wine from California I have come across.

This wine has a really interesting nose, almost like fruit punch. I feel like I'm at a high school party and one of the cool football guys poured cheap vodka in the punch. However, there is a great underlying complexity, with a really interesting lingering Bloody Mary component. It has the tomato juice, the Tabasco, even a little celery stalk, which makes the aroma really compelling. The flavor of this wine is just really clever. I am wowed by the floral component, with lilac and lavender flavors, followed by secondary flavors of blueberry jam.

Palate Primer:

Tabasco Sauce

Created by Edmund McIlhenny in 1868, Tabasco Sauce continues to be produced on Avery Island, Louisiana, in the traditional way. The sauce is created by fermenting mashed peppers in oak barrels for up to three years, and shows layers of complex flavors in addition to the legendary heat.

Montevina, Terra d'Oro Teroldego, 2006; $13
Amador County, California
Grape: Teroldego
14.2% ABV
500 cases produced
www.montevina.com

My attraction to this wine is doubly surprising because I have not normally liked a lot of wines from Montevina. There is a huge lesson here: with wine, it pays to continue tasting and keep an open mind. I always tell people, "Just because you've had one or two Chardonnays you did not like does not mean you hate all Chardonnay. Dude, there are millions!" And just because I've had like seven or eight wines from Montevina that I did not think were up to snuff does not mean I hate all Montevina. In fact, I would totally enjoy this with some barbecue ribs and I think it could last three to five years in the cellar.

This is an Italian varietal wine from California that completely brings the thunder, and it comes from a winery that has totally exceeded my expectations. Now, that's the sort of surprise I can't wait to share.

Meet the Grape: Teroldego

Native to the Alto Adige region in Northeast Italy, Teroldego has found little success outside of its home territory and has only one approved region in Italy: Teroldego Rotaliano DOC. Teroldego has been shown to be a relative of Syrah, and with low tannins and high potential alcohol, its wines often draw flavor comparisons to Zinfandel.

NOTE TO SELF: DRINK THIS

This wine reminds me that I sometimes have to heed some of my own advice. In terms of red wines, I am addicted to Petit Verdot, and as far as white, I absolutely go to Pernand-Vergelesses—a Premier Cru of Burgundy. It's not one of the great names, like all those "Montrachets," and few people talk about these wines. Even I have sort of neglected them—but that is a mistake on my part, and it's about to change.

This wine is shockingly good. I tasted it head-to-head with several Grand Cru white Burgundies that cost ten times as much, and everything about this wine screamed top-notch Burgundy to me. It is very clean, very expressive, with nutmeg, walnut, and almond components on the mid-palate, which give way to a beautiful toasty Grape-Nuts cereal and a touch of movie theater butter. There is also a hint of pear, followed by guava, kiwi, and starfruit that are elegant yet explosive. This is what Chardonnay can do when done properly.

Palate Primer:

Grape-Nuts

Created in 1897 by Charles W. Post in Battle Creek, Michigan, Grape-Nuts does not contain grapes or nuts. However, the flavor is both grainy and nutty due to the cereal's manufacture in an old-fashioned gas-fired oven. Post added "Grape" to the name because the cereal was sweetened with maltose, which was commonly called grape sugar.

Maison Louis Jadot Pernand-Vergelesses Blanc Premier Cru Clos de la Croix de Pierre, 2006; $30

AOC Pernand-Vergelesses Premier Cru, Bourgogne, France

Grape: Chardonnay

13.5% ABV

300 cases imported

www.louisjadot.com

This is very food-friendly stuff, but the one thing I am most craving with this is mushroom soup. That's right: mushroom soup. Tell me I'm crazy, because I'm not scared. I bet if you try this pairing you'll be blown away. This wine almost has a little truffle component on the mid-palate that is really going to marry perfectly with other earthy, mushroomy flavors.

This wine is so good, so exotic, and off the radar that I am stunned at what a great value it is. Plus, this marks another Louis Jadot wine on my list. It really goes to show that there are great values everywhere from untapped regions and unlikely producers, which is why it's vital to always keep an open mind. I really hope you'll find this wine, try it, and remember the amazing qualities of Pernand-Vergelesses. I'm making a promise to myself that I will.

wine country

Pernand-Vergelesses lies on the western side of Burgundy's Côte de Beaune, bordered by Savigny-lès-Beaune to the south, and by Aloxe-Corton to the east. The commune produces mostly red wine from Pinot Noir grapes, along with a smaller amount of white. The name Pernand is derived from the French *perdu*, meaning "lost," and *nand*, meaning "spring," as an underground water source.

CHÂTEAUNEUF GOES SUNBATHING

In New York City, all people talk about is real estate. I'm sure Californians would be bored with our talk of condo boards, rent control, and parking. In wine country, I feel like all people want to talk about is the weather. Just breathe a whisper about Bordeaux and you get the whole, "Well, they don't have this weather, eh? Look at that sunshine." That's all I hear out there! And that's all great, but why in God's name do they not just let the weather do the work? They already have this amazing winemaking climate, and yet they feel a need to bulk up, ink up, overextract, and manipulate the fruit.

That's where this wine really succeeds. It lets the weather do the work and the fruit speak for itself. Edmunds St. John is a really fun producer, and I bow down to Steve Edmunds for crafting a wine that is a worthy tribute to Châteauneuf-du-Pape, offering just a little more fruit and little bolder style without seeming fake or manipulated.

I am really feeling this aroma! It smells like strawberries drowning in Aunt Jemima pancake syrup. It is actually one of the most obvious examples of maple syrup I've ever smelled in a wine, along with little

Label Lore

"Rocks and Gravel" is an allusion to Steve Edmunds's philosophy of making wines through which "the earth speaks." His similarly named Shell and Bone White features Viognier and Roussanne grapes grown on ancient seabeds of limestone and clay.

Edmunds St. John, Rocks and Gravel, 2004; $16
California
Grapes: Grenache (38%), Mourvèdre (34%), Syrah (28%)
14.5% ABV
800 cases produced
www.edmundsstjohn.com

hints of clove and some rocks and dirt. On the palate, the fruit is really pretty, with the Grenache just singing with strawberries and pepper. If I were trying to identify this wine in a blind tasting, I would be betting Rhône on this every time, which is a huge compliment. It achieves extraordinary Old World flavors from a New World place, which makes it very captivating to me. There is not even a prestigious region on the label: Since the grapes are sourced from all over, including Paso Robles, Sonoma, and El Dorado County, it just says "California."

This is Châteauneuf-du-Pape-esque in every way except the one we can do without: price. True Châteauneuf is going to be in the $30 to $40 range. With this wine, you get a similar flavor profile, texture, and sophistication for half the price. That irresistible combination makes this not only one of the most exciting 101 wines, but one of the best buys of the list. Kudos, kudos, kudos to these guys!

NO IMITATION

You've probably tasted the worst of Chablis—a gallon jug of California wine made from Colombard or even Thompson's Seedless table grapes. This stuff is not Chablis at all. It's produced by name-pirates like Paul Masson, Inglenook, and Peter Vella, who are the fat-cat equivalents of fake Louis Vuitton bag sellers on Canal Street. These guys know better, but continue to capitalize on centuries of excellence from wine regions like Chablis. It's time you take a huge leap forward and taste the best of Chablis, an all-Chardonnay wine from the chilly northern reaches of Burgundy.

Verget is one of the great producers in all of Burgundy, and this wine comes from the most famous of the seven Grand Cru vineyards of Chablis, Les Clos. It benefits from the cool climate of the region (Chablis is closer to Champagne than it is to most of Burgundy) and from the soils rich in fossilized shells and limestone.

These soils give this wine an amazing mineral, blue-stone, flinty aroma. I feel like Frodo in *The Lord of the Rings*, trying to start a fire by striking a couple of rocks together. Where is that Gandalf when you need him? There is also a real cereal component to this wine; I'm going to go with Kellogg's Corn Flakes.

On the palate, it is extremely clean with a gorgeous mouthfeel, and some serious richness on the mid-palate transitions to a zesty pear-infused-with-mango finish. This is a full-bodied, serious white. If you are up for an outside-the-box pairing, here is a gorgeous white

La Maison Verget, Les Clos Chablis, 2006; $84
AOC Grand Cru Chablis, France
Grape: Chardonnay
www.verget-sa.com

wine that will match up to steak as readily as fish. This wine really shows the potential of the 2006 vintage and will last five to seven years easily.

In terms of flavor and intrigue, there is no comparison between this wine and the Cali imitators. Of course the price follows. At over $80 a bottle, a jug-size helping of this stuff would be a car payment for many people. However, like so many of the European wines in this book, prices are only going up. In December, Chablis producer Michel Laroche predicted we will see brutal price increases in Chablis, because grape costs are up 20 percent, adding that the price of Pinot Noir in southern France was up 60 percent. Patronize the pirates for your DVDs and your knockoff Burberry scarf if you must, but please, not for your Chablis.

Palate Primer:

Flint

Also called flintstone, flint is a sedimentary form of quartz, usually gray, black, or dark brown in color. Because of its ability to flake to a sharp edge, flint was used in toolmaking in the Stone Age, and when struck against steel, it can produce a spark capable of lighting a fire. In wine, flint is a common descriptor of mineral flavors.

PARTNERS IN WINE

This Pinot comes from a fairly small winery established in 1995 in Santa Barbara County by Geoff and Alison Rusack. The winemaking team at Rusack, John and Helen Falcone, is also a husband-and-wife team. John spent time as head winemaker at Atlas Peak Vineyards, and Helen worked previously at Chimney Rock, so you add all this up and you get a lot of talent and a lot of passion going into every bottle. Believe me—you can taste it.

The nose of this Pinot shows really gorgeous raspberry as well as some late-autumn leaves, just as they are starting to turn brown and drop. There is a beautiful secondary whiff of cranberry lurking beneath the earthy foliage. It is obviously very well crafted from the start.

However, it is the golden elegance on the palate that separates this wine from so many others I've tasted from this region. First, there are these very fascinating black olive and green olive flavors woven throughout the wine, bringing to it a sophisticated edge. The hallmark

Label Lore

The labels of Rusack wine feature images of Catalina tiles, handcrafted and highly collectible tiles that form one of the artistic legacies of the California Arts and Crafts movement. The image was chosen as a tribute to Alison Rusack's great-grandparents, who operated a ceramics factory on Santa Catalina Island, just off the southern California coast.

Rusack, Santa Rita Hills Pinot Noir Reserve, 2006; $40

Santa Rita Hills, California
Grape: Pinot Noir
14.5% ABV
496 cases produced
www.rusack.com

wine country

Santa Rita Hills is an AVA of approximately 100 square miles. Located between the towns of Buellton and Lompoc in Santa Barbara County, the cool climate appellation takes its name from the Santa Ynez River, which intersects it.
www.staritahills.com

of great Pinot is its silky-smooth texture, and this wine puts it on like a Valentine's negligee. The supple strawberry flavors really separate this wine from the pretenders, with great length and explosiveness of fruit. The texture is like velvet, and the flavors finish with an obvious plum component—round, ripe plums.

The finish on this wine lasts a solid minute—not a New York minute but a West Coast minute—because these flavors are really taking their time. And on the finish, violets and rose petals are flitting around my mouth.

This wine is really the complete package that I love to see in a New World Pinot Noir. It has that freshness of fruit and brightness that makes it distinctly California, yet remains true to the elegance and refinement of Burgundy. Apparently two can not only tango, but also craft a truly fantastic glass of wine.

#79 A PINOT TASTE TEST

Do you like the taste of Pinot Noir? Do you know what Pinot Noir is *really*? For many post-*Sideways* Pinot fans, Pinot Noir exists only as the candy-coated bulk Pinot or over-extracted, blended Frankenstein Pinot that California producers have been doling out. If you are trying to decide exactly what Pinot Noir is and if you like it, this wine can be your benchmark. With great balance and a huge amount of OS (obnoxious silkiness), this wine shows what properly made Pinot can achieve.

It also has the interesting nose that Pinot is renowned for. There is a clever creaminess here, like cottage cheese meets cherries with beautiful hints of watermelon coming through. This wine is very aromatically inclined, with a little hint of Brussels sprouts on the tail end that makes it slightly vegetal and extremely exciting.

The supple, silky texture of this wine is incredibly seductive. I think that for relatively new wine drinkers, the idea that a wine can be this flavorful and this smooth will be a huge smack to the head. That, again, is the beauty of Pinot Noir. The flavor is a smorgasbord

VAYNERCABULARY

OS (n)—Obnoxious Silkiness. *A trait that certain wines may demonstrate in their texture on the palate. Pinot Noir, with its soft tannins, often embodies obnoxious silkiness. In addition, well-aged Merlot, Cabernet Sauvignon, and Bordeaux blends are candidates to show OS.*

Arista, Russian River Valley Pinot Noir, 2005; $45
Russian River Valley, California
Grape: Pinot Noir
14.2% ABV
600 cases produced
www.aristawinery.com

Meet the Grape: Pinot Noir

Pinot Noir has a reputation for being a difficult grape to grow and vinify—but also as one of the most sophisticated and rewarding wines for wine lovers. Pinot Noir is synonymous with the red wines of Burgundy, but more recently Oregon, British Columbia, New Zealand, and cooler areas of California show promise for the fickle grape. Pinot Noir is known for making complex, earthy wines that are full-bodied but not heavy or tannic.

of cherries, everything from black cherries to Maraschino. And the hints of white pepper bouncing around in my mouth make this enormously complex and exciting. I believe this wine is better than a lot of the Pinot Noirs scoring 90-plus points from major critics. It will last for five to ten years easily in the cellar, and over the next thirty-six months should really hit its stride.

In terms of food, I want to have rabbit with this wine. Like cherry sauce, which is found on top of rabbit a lot, I think this wine's huge blend of cherry flavors would be a perfect companion. The flavors are so long and impressive, I am in complete love with this wine, and with Pinot Noir. Allow me to introduce you, you might just love real Pinot too.

BY GEORGE, YOU'VE GOT IT

Fox Gordon is a project of Natasha Mooney, one of the great woman winemakers—make that one of the great winemakers—of Australia. Before creating Fox Gordon, Mooney made her mark on the global wine scene with several vintages of Barossa Valley Estates E&E Black Pepper Shiraz, an iconic and critically lauded wine. It's unfortunate that wineries owned and operated by women are unusual. However, this wine from Mooney and her partners—Jane Gordon and Rachel Atkins—makes my list on merit alone.

First, I appreciate this wine for its sheer innovation. Australia is not at the forefront of most Americans' minds when it comes to Cabernet or Tempranillo, so making a blend of the two is a big gamble. The nose of this wine is very, very tight. It's difficult to discern many flavors, and it is actually one of the weaker noses on the list. There is some dull, subtle blueberry and raspberry, along with a cedar box component.

On the palate, however, this wine more than makes amends, unleashing cranberry fruit integrated with white pepper and a hint

Label Lore

In keeping with their family-friendly approach to wine, the name By George is a tribute to Jane Gordon's son. Other wines from Fox Gordon include Abby Viognier, named for Rachel Atkins's daughter, and Eight Uncles Shiraz.

of green beans. It really makes me think of Thanksgiving dinner. The flavors are really fascinating, with bright fruit and a hint of oakiness, but it is the cranberry that rules the day. If you are the Thanksgiving guest who loves to slather that cranberry relish on everything, you *have* to get this wine. It has a great viscous mouthfeel, but it is more than a fruit bomb—which makes it a great representation of a different type of wine from Australia.

This wine is actually more Bordeaux-like than Australian—interesting, sophisticated, very polished, and well made. It also offers good value: In flavor and price, it walks the line between easy-drinking and serious wine. If you are the average Joe, who enjoys NASCAR and taking your dog out in the woods and shooting a deer—but you like wine—you don't have to drink Yellow Tail. You can drink serious stuff for a reasonable price. This is a real man's wine—one that just happens to be made by women.

A BOLD BET IN BORDEAUX

One thing I strongly believe in is legacy. And, in order to achieve legacy, I am putting down some bold predictions throughout this book for all to see. I want to be like Jimmy "The Greek" Snyder—not in the sense that he said some wild stuff on TV, but in the way the guy was never afraid to take a long shot or announce his predictions to the world. Hmm, maybe Nostradamus is a better example.

Anyway, here goes: Château Valrose will one day be considered one of the premier estates of Saint-Estèphe. As a dedicated fan of this Château, I believe they are a profound, up-and-coming producer and that in the next decade or two, people will be mentioning them in the same breath as other Saint-Estèphe greats like Château Cos d'Estournel. How's that for a bold prediction for a wine that sells for 20 bucks?

To describe the nose of this wine, I need to create a fantasy dinner for you: You know what stuffed peppers look like? Imagine you're having stuffed cherries. They are cherries the size of peppers, burst-

---

VAYNERCABULARY

Workman's wine (n)—*A wine that shows structure, strength, and power, usually with some presence of masculine, Old World flavors. A workman's wine, whether red or white, shows generous body and matches well with hearty foods; it's the type of wine you enjoy after a day on the tractor.*

Château Valrose, Cuvée Alienor, 2004; $30
AOC Saint-Estèphe, Bordeaux, France
Grapes: Merlot (50%), Cabernet Sauvignon (40%),
    Cabernet Franc (10%)
13% ABV
1,200 cases imported
www.bobbofman.com

wine country

The wine commune of Saint-Estèphe is located on the left bank of the Gironde River in Bordeaux's Haut-Médoc district. Cabernet Sauvignon typically dominates the blend in this region, making this wine somewhat atypical.

ing with Stove Top stuffing. And, there is crème fraîche on top. Now there's a crazy image.

Ready for another one? I took a taste of this wine, and it was like Mike Ditka spoke to me in a dream. His mustache was dripping red, and he told me he loves this wine. It's a workman's red wine—a spectacular throwback, strong and integrated. There are both New World and Old World flavors in here, so you have cherries, raspberries, and plum juice colliding with jalapeño peppers, cabbage, and pickle juice. I love the brilliant contradiction of two Bordeaux flavor profiles, and to top it all off, a massive bitter—yes, bitter—tannic component.

This wine really needs a big fat slab of steak to take off that bitter edge. It is inky, black, concentrated, and complex. You would be very hard-pressed to find these types of flavors, this sort of backbone and structure, in California Cabernet or Aussie Shiraz. This is a spectacular red wine lover's red wine, and I am putting my money on this estate as a big winner in Bordeaux.

FROZEN JUICE CONCENTRATE

Only a few wine regions on earth excel at making natural ice wine, a process in which grapes are allowed to freeze on the vine to concentrate the sugars and flavors before pressing. New Zealand is not one of them. However, by artificially freezing the juice and separating the ice, Selaks has been producing this high-tech ice wine consistently for twenty-two vintages. The Germans and Canadians might consider it cheating, but I'd say these Kiwis have it down.

Another advantage to artificial freezing (cryoextraction, for you techies) is the wine is far more affordable to produce. Because true ice wines requires hand harvesting, complete with the threat of frostbite and arctic animals, traditional Canadian and German versions often approach 100 bucks for a tiny

Label Lore

The U.S. Bureau of Alcohol, Tobacco and Firearms has determined that in order for a wine to be called "icewine" in the U.S., the grapes must be at least partially frozen on the vine. Germany and Canada are the two most recognized producers of icewine, and frigid temperatures and night harvesting make naturally frozen fruit the standard. In Germany and Austria, the style is often spelled *eiswein*. Wines from regions where the grapes do not freeze on the vine may use the term "ice wine," as two words, or alternatives like "vin de glace."

Selaks, Premium Selection Ice Wine, 2006; $18
East Coast, New Zealand
Grapes: Gewürztraminer (51%), Riesling (49%)
10% ABV
4,000 cases imported
www.nobilo.co.nz

bottle. They generally may have more complexity and nuance, but also represent a huge leap in price from this wine, which is about the cost of lunch for one at Così.

I'm very excited about including several dessert wines on this list, and—go figure—one of them is a non-traditional ice wine from New Zealand. First, the tangerines and oranges are just so obvious and exciting on the nose that they really pull you in. The aroma is very citrusy, clean, vibrant, and bouncy. In addition to the tangerine and orange, this has a very distinct ginger component that I really like.

Now for a taste: Hello pineapple! Hello papaya! Hello mango! I think I got on the wrong flight and wound up in Hawaii instead of New Zealand. The flavor is just so candied and loaded with sweet tropical fruit. Ironically, I think we're only missing kiwi for this to be my perfect dessert wine. It is really delicious stuff, a great alternative to what's out there and a great value as well. The other thing I really like about this is that it's actually medium-bodied, not real sticky or syrupy. It's almost like a fortified version of a Moscato d'Asti, just a little more syrupy and without the bubbles. This wine will last for three to seven years, but there's no need to wait; it's vibrant, youthful, and delicious right now.

HOT STUFF FROM BAROLO

Abig problem with the world, and not just the wine world, is how everything is becoming more the same. Culture, people, and tastes are all becoming homogenized. And there is nothing more discouraging to me than to drink a Barolo that tastes like California Syrah. So, I have to give this wine the nod for really embracing tradition and portraying what Barolo is all about, while also being approachable and likable for many people.

The 2003 vintage in Europe was an unusually hot one, and a lot of winemakers, from Italy to Bordeaux, made very over-the-top, *non-traditional* wines. This Barolo kept its hold on tradition. There is a really intense peppermint and spearmint component on the nose, along with some towering evergreen trees, like hiking in the shadowy forest outside Seattle. There is also some dried tomato and some of that V8 juice that you know I love so much, along with some curious oil, gasoline, metal-shop aromas. In a word—rustic.

In the flavor, there is some meaty venison and leather, and on the

VAYNERCABULARY

Manipulated (adj)—*having been altered in the winery, often by technological means, to change the flavor of the wine. The addition of wood chips, sugar, acids, color, or enzymes, as well as the removal of alcohol, are types of manipulation that may have beneficial or deleterious effects, depending on your perspective and palate.*

Ascheri, Barolo Vigna dei Pola, 2003; $59

DOCG Barolo, Piedmonte, Italy
Grape: Nebbiolo
14.5% ABV
1,400 cases produced
www.ascherivini.it

palate the wine is very, very dry. It is just totally mouth-puckering and really clings to your palate, with all its pretty sour cherries and obvious blackberry coming through. It is quite pure and quite rich, without crossing the line. In fact, I would say this wine shows a real lack of manipulation, which is exactly how it should be. This is a throwback to classic Barolo.

However, because of the vintage, this wine is a friendly introduction to the classic style. That hot 2003 vintage gave this wine a little bit of New World love, which serves it really well. It almost reminds me of the great 1997 vintage, which was also hot and very ripe. All together, it equals a classic portrayal of a wine that a lot of people will enjoy, especially with food. I am about to go running for a chunk of Parmesan, because the dryness of this wine screams for food. It may not be a wine to drink by itself, but it's one you're going to love drinking.

A RIVER RUNS THROUGH IT

In the vineyards of Austria, white grapes rule, accounting for 70 percent of the production. And the king of these grapes is Grüner Veltliner, or as we like to call it in the nerddom of wine: GrüVee. In addition to making great-quality white wines, the Austrians seem incredibly generous with them, and quite a few GrüVees have come on the market in bargain 1-liter bottles. They really need to come up with a laundry detergent marketing program, like a bottle-necker that screams, "New larger size. 33% more wine!"

Beyond merely representing great value, I believe these wines have the potential to become a very important white varietal wine in the American market. These wines are clean and fresh, and just as you've seen New Zealand Sauvignon Blanc explode in the U.S., I think you may see Austrian Grüner Veltliner follow. Most notably, this Austrian white is very, very food-friendly, with plenty of acidity from the cool vineyards along the iconic Danube River.

On the aroma, this wine has a distinct graininess, almost like a bowl of Grape-Nuts cereal on the nose, along with an imaginary splash of lemon and lime. It is very bright, with almost a fresh-cut grass smell. The cereal quality and nuttiness are very obvious, with a heavy dose of walnuts and chestnuts coming through.

In flavor, this wine is very dry with a ton of acidity that grabs the outer perimeter of your palate in a very exciting way. This big acid attack and fresh flavor yearns for charred fish. Give me black bass!

Sollner Danubio, Grüner Veltliner, 2006; $13
Wagrum, Austria
Grape: Grüner Veltliner
11.5% ABV
166 cases imported
www.danubio.cc

wine country

Small production wines like this one are very typical for Austria, which includes over 20,000 small wine-producing estates, most of whom sell their wine on the premises. Large wine estates, over 500 acres, are very rare in Austria.
www.winesfromaustria.com

Give me salmon! Give me monkfish! Long after I've swallowed this wine, the long, acidic finish just keeps on coming, with this interesting gooseberry component. Part of me hates to use the term "grapes" when describing a wine. It feels like cheating. But this wine just comes across as good old-fashioned green grapes, with the nutty flavors integrated throughout really providing some character. Who doesn't love a mouthful of liquid nuts?

If you are a person who usually chooses Sauvignon Blanc and Pinot Grigio over Chardonnay, you are clearly drawn to acidic, clean, fresh wine, and I think if you give this a shot, it may quickly rise to the top of your list.

AN ANTIDOTE FOR THE HATER-ADE

This wine is not exactly a well-kept secret. Robert Parker turned me on to Clio many years ago, and I've been drinking it ever since. So, I have to give kudos to Bob because this is one of his fruit bombs that I can totally latch on to and enjoy.

This deep red wine has a really nice ground beef, almost a roast beef aroma to it, along with some fresh-cracked black pepper, not that crap you get in a metal box. Then there is this really pretty, quite obvious goji berry, and also some lovely cranberry on the nose. The purity and integrity of the fruit in this wine is really just exceptional. It is almost dizzying; I might go into a fruit coma. Following the fruit, there is this gorgeous bacon fat aroma that is extremely attractive and brings great dimension to the wine. If you want to talk New World, cutting-edge—this is it! For all the Mac users, the early adopters, the people who went out and bought Laserdisc players in the 1990s and were dialing up on the Internet on 2,400-band

Palate Primer:

Goji Berry

Also known as a wolfberry, goji berry is the English name for a bright orange berry grown primarily in China. The berries are often sold dried and are similar in size and texture to a small raisin, but with varying levels of sweetness and flavors that may include nuances of cherry, plum, and earth. The berries are especially popular for their antioxidant properties.

Bodegas El Nido, Clio, 2006; $45
DOCa Jumilla, Spain
Grapes: Monastrell (70%), Cabernet Sauvignon (30%)
15.5% ABV
1,100 cases imported

modems, this is the wine you want in order to stay edgy and ahead of the curve.

The fruit is beautifully integrated on the palate and it makes a seamless segue from the early fruit to the mid-palate. As I continue to sip it, I am just blown away by the overall complexity of this wine and its complete richness with exotic cloves, sweet red and yellow fruit, and loads of oak and cherries.

You *could* drink this by yourself, watching the game on a Sunday afternoon, but with all this monster fruit, ripeness, and alcohol, you'd be headed for a nappy-nap real quick. I think this wine is really made for big foods—steak, pasta, game. With all its lusciousness, explosiveness, and power, this is the wine I want on hand at a pig roast. However, it's not just a fruit bomb. There is power here, but it's also coupled with elegance and complexity.

So, I'm not going to caution you Old World wine lovers like you might expect. Instead, I am instructing you to try this wine. If you're the person who hates the ripe New World fruit bombs (and you've been drinking on that hater-ade) try this wine. No matter what your taste, you cannot deny that this wine is complex, thoughtful, and well made.

SUPER UMBRIAN

I f you can imagine a map of the Italian boot and then drop a pushpin right in the center, you know where this wine comes from. Being centrally located, this part of Umbria became a strategic place for travelers between Rome and the Holy Land, so the Sovereign Military Order of Malta stuck a castle here around the year 1150 as a stopover place. The Order is headquartered in Rome, and to this day has its own passports, stamps, currency, and, of course, wine.

With a blend of grapes that is both international (i.e., French) and Italian, this wine is what I would call a Super-Umbrian. On the nose, I get a nice peppermint-spearmint component along with some really beautiful blackberry flavors coming through. There are also hints of black cherry and rhubarb, along with a little of that sweaty sock, armpit aroma. There is definitely something masculine going on here. It's like a bunch of 18-year-old guys just got done playing basketball and hit the showers, but instead of water, out came a whole fruit punch of fresh juices.

VAYNERCABULARY:

Grape Ape wine (n)—*A Grape Ape wine is one that would delight the Grape Ape, the star of* The Great Grape Ape *produced by Hanna-Barbera Productions and broadcast on ABC beginning in 1975. The unmistakable Grape Ape is a purple gorilla standing forty feet tall who, above all else, loves the flavor of grapes.*

Castello di Magione Morcinaia, Colli del Trasimeno, 2004; $22

DOC Colli del Trasimeno, Umbria, Italy
Grapes: Merlot (40%), Cabernet Sauvignon (40%), Sangiovese (20%)
14% ABV
540 cases produced
www.castellodimagione.it

There is really pretty pomegranate fruit on the palate, along with ripe grapey flavors. This is a total Grape Ape wine. It's almost like an Aussie-Italian hybrid. Their mascot should be a kangaroo bouncing around in a blue and white Italia soccer jersey, because this has the great ripe fruit of the Barossa Valley along with the balance and depth that make Italian wine so interesting and exciting.

The finish is very pretty and delivers its blackberry-chocolate flavors with pinpoint accuracy, followed by a charcoal finish and this absolutely gorgeous length. While this wine tastes great now, it will only get more serious and sophisticated over the next five to seven years. And now that the traveler-guarding business has slowed, the Order dedicates their time and profits to global charitable organizations, providing hospitals and humanitarian aid, making this wine a great way to spend 20 bucks. And you won't even need Sovereign Military Order of Malta currency to pick it up.

RISING STAR

You know those great actors that never quite make it to the A-list, but every time you see them on-screen, you know the film is going to be great? Anderson's Conn Valley is that guy.

This producer does not get the red carpet attention of the Napa big boys—Caymus, Montelena, Cakebread—but it also does not command their triple-digit price tags, which places it firmly on my list of great values. I first fell in love with Anderson's Conn Valley back in the early 1990s. It was actually pretty hot back then, but has somehow managed to stay just far enough outside the mainstream, like an indie film actor content to make art for art's sake.

On the aroma, this Cab is just a beautiful pepper bomb. I'm talking bell peppers—in hues of red and green and yellow. There is also a Heinz ketchup component. And when it comes to Heinz, I really

---

Science Experiment:	Temperature Control

Most people drink their whites too cold and their reds too warm. Wines really show their greatest diversity of flavors when enjoyed at a temperature that reveals them without emphasizing the alcohol, about 45° for most whites and 55° for most reds. Observe the impact of temperature on flavor by tasting the same wine at several different temperatures.

Anderson's Conn Valley Vineyards, Napa Valley Cabernet Sauvignon Estate Reserve, 2005; $68

Napa Valley, California
Grape: Cabernet Sauvignon
15.1% ABV
3,406 cases produced
www.connvalleyvineyards.com

do like that tomato ketchup flavor, even though Heinz Field in Pittsburgh has left a bad taste in my mouth ever since the Jets' heart-breaking AFC playoff loss there. Beautiful, nicely rounded blueberry fruit aromas follow through in the flavor.

And man, does this have great flavor! It is extremely elegant, rounded, and polished, with a great balance of fruit and woody oak, some green leaves, and these sour, *sour* cherries on the mid-palate. The flavors are long and polished, with the beauty and profoundness to rival great Cabernet-based wines from anywhere in the world. On the finish, there is this great flavor of English peas. The peas are subtle and refined and really add intrigue to the blueberry fruit. This wine will drink well over the next eight to ten years. If you're the person who only goes to Tom Cruise blockbusters, it's time to be a little more adventurous and take notice of some new talent. Because there is no doubt in my mind that this wine is capable of standing eye to eye with Jordan, Far Niente, Duckhorn, or any of those iconic Napa names and totally stealing the scene.

A SPOONFUL OF SUGAR

wine country

> The Gippsland Wine Zone is located on the southeastern tip of mainland Australia in the province of Victoria. It stretches from Phillip Island in the west to the border of New South Wales in the east.

Pinot Gris makes some of the most interesting wines in the world, especially in Oregon and Alsace, where this grape absolutely thrives. In fact, the only way to make this wine more intriguing might be to cultivate the grape biodynamically in volcanic soils in the southeast corner of Australia, then ferment the unfiltered juice in barrels using naturally occurring wild yeast. That is precisely how winemaker Neil Prentice creates this amazing white wine.

The first thing about this wine that got my attention is the obvious touch of sweetness. It has seven grams of sugar per liter, which is more than twice the amount in most dry table wines. The inefficiency of permitting wild yeasts to act on the wine, rather than adding cultured yeast, means some extra sugar remains in the wine naturally. On the nose, melon meets sugar cubes and a little bit of candy cane. It's not quite as pepperminty as a candy cane, but there is a hint of that fresh sweetness. Overall, this is really pretty, with obvious cantaloupe and melon.

This wine is gorgeously light, fresh, and friendly in the mouth, with a real flower component. I am also getting some St. John's wort. If you have ever included St. John's wort in tea, like my family does,

Moondarra Vineyard, Holly's Garden Pinot Gris, 2006; $20

Gippsland, Australia
Grape: Pinot Gris
13.5% ABV
2,000 cases produced

you'll recognize its interesting, distinctive flavor in this Pinot Gris. There is also a lively grapefruit component with that sweetness coming through like powdered sugar over waffles. The sweetness here may be a little more than many wine drinkers are used to, but that little innovation brings a lot of possibility with food.

I think this wine would work really great with the naturally sweet meat and mineral flavors of Maryland stone crabs. And, it would do simply amazing things with foie gras. A lot of people serve Sauternes or other dessert wines with foie gras, but this has enough sweetness to step up and do some real damage! I believe that as this wine ages, over the next two to three years, it is only going to get more complex, adding petrol components. I totally embrace this wine for its originality, and serving up that little shot of sugar that we all want. It might not suit everyone, but a few people are going to be writing me love letters over this wine.

BE VERY AFRAID

Ever had a Sagrantino? I didn't think so. Sagrantino is grown almost exclusively around the small town of Montefalco in Umbria, and is also superexpensive, which pretty much equals "no sales in America." Oh, and it's so opaque, so dark and foreboding, that it looks like black paint. Forget Super Tuscans and big Barolos—this is the real Italian bad boy. And I believe that as this grape earns serious respect, you're going to see it bully its way onto more restaurant wine lists in the coming years.

The aroma of this inky wine is like roasted peppers meet Grandma's spice rack. Now, Grammy came from the Old Country, and she never threw anything away, so she had hundreds of dusty spice bottles. They are all in here—black pepper, cloves, oregano—especially if they were on sale. Speaking of dust, there is a really interesting dusty grapes element. It's like your pops was in the garage building your soapbox derby car and got his sawdust all over a bowl of black grapes, but you just grabbed a bunch and ate them anyway.

This is a P^3 wine! That stands for power, profoundness, and polish. On the palate, there is enormous structure plus ungodly amounts of roasted pepper flavors with this cinnamon component dancing through the mid-palate. The tannin level is absolutely off the charts. It is really too big for anything except your most massive slab of meat. I am talking Fred Flintstone Brontosaurus burger, ribs-that-flip-the-car-over meat. With this kind of tannin and structure, I

Madonna Alta, Sagrantino di Montefalco, 2004; $60
DOCG Sagrantino di Montefalco, Italy
Grape: Sagrantino
14% ABV
500 cases imported
www.madonnalta.it

expect this wine to last fifteen to twenty-five years easily. This is aggressive, savage, brutal stuff. I would take great pleasure sticking this bottle in a room with some California Cabernet and Barossa Valley Shiraz just so I could watch them tremble.

But I see the potential for real greatness here. By 2010 this wine will be getting more approachable, and by 2020 you'll be ready to drink this at your daughter's wedding. You'll be calling me from the reception to tell me how cool I am. So buy this Sagrantino now. You have at least a decade to build up the courage to open it.

Meet the Grape: Sagrantino

Cultivated almost exclusively in the DOCG Sagrantino di Montefalco, this grape is traditionally vinified into sweet red wine. The thick skins of the grape give it good resistance to disease and pests, as well as potent tannins for the production of powerful dry red wine.

MY, WHAT A BIG PINOT YOU HAVE

I've spent some time ridiculing Pinot Noirs like this one. When it comes to Pinot, I don't demand to be able to watch a Jets game through the glass, but I like to be able to see my fingers. I am not saying this particular wine has Petit Sirah in it like so many of them do, but it certainly appears to be one of those Pinot bastard children—hugely extracted, inky, and Darth Vader–dark. The only surprise is, this wine is utterly refined and downright delicious.

Despite having the muscle of a Romanian gymnast, this wine has not been doped with Petit Sirah and put through Cold War–era Olympic training in the winery. Rather, owner Adam Tolmach spends his time crafting this wine in the vineyard. When 2005 looked like it was bound to be a bumper crop, Tolmach went through the vineyard culling fruit, adjusting the crop, and carefully trimming to get the right amount of fruit and sunlight on each vine. The result is a wine that has intensity and sincerity.

The aroma offers classic dark raspberries along with tires and skid

---

VAYNERCABULARY

Skid mark (n)—*A mark left by a rubber tire when a wheel loses traction on the surface of the road, usually due to braking or extreme maneuvering. In wine, a skid mark flavor includes hints of hot rubber and asphalt, and could be big, as in a tractor-trailer skid, or subtle, as in a bicycle skid. Pinot Noir and Pinotage often show skid mark aromas.*

Ojai, Pinot Noir Clos Pepe Vineyard, 2005; $52
Santa Rita Hills, California
Grapes: Pinot Noir
14% ABV
642 cases produced
www.ojaivineyard.com

marks, like the General Lee just tore out of a raspberry patch. There is also some very pretty burnt wood and this lardy, bacon fat flavor on the nose that is really intriguing.

On the palate, this Pinot has everything you could ask for in a fruit bomb of a wine. I really enjoy the inkiness, the mouthfeel, and the structure, which is often lacking in this type of wine. The cherry and strawberry flavors are really specific and well defined. They don't get muddied or meld together. To add intrigue, there is a little cinnamon stick and some cedar. This wine is so delicious and so massive, I want to bite the glass and chew on it. It has the structure to last three to five years in the cellar, and it has the guts to stand up to not just game and lamb, but even a juicy steak.

It's a rare occurrence, but I am running out of adjectives worthy of this wine. We can start with: amazing, tremendous, phenomenal. This is not the style of Pinot that normally excites me, but this is a wine that will satisfy both the fruit bomb fans and the lovers of nuance.

BORDEAUX GOES BLANC

In your mind, right now, I want you to picture a glass of Bordeaux. Can you see it? Okay, now tell me what color it is. I am betting that your glass was red. It's okay—so was mine. Yet, in this area of Bordeaux, Graves, there is almost as much white wine as there is red. And Château Latour-Martillac is classified as a top Château for both their red wine and their white.

It's time that we all take notice that white Bordeaux can be truly exceptional. These blends of Sauvignon Blanc and Sémillon are among the most interesting, weighty, and crisp whites in the world.

This particular wine has beautiful melon, cantaloupe, and papaya dancing around on the mid-palate, finishing with a gorgeous lemon-lime-Sprite-7UP-Squirt component. By keeping the wine on its lees (which is just a fancy word for "dying yeast") for over a year and bottling in dark bottles, this Château makes whites that will outlast some red wines in the cellar. The length and mouthfeel of this wine would rival any great Viognier from the Rhône. And the cleanness and crispness could go toe-to-toe with a Sancerre. This wine is that good!

Something about this wine makes me feel like I am on an Alaskan cruise. It is like watching a waterfall, with all this weight and impact and grandeur, yet washes across my mouth so clean and crisp. This is the sort of great wine that the Europeans keep to themselves. They are drinking these white Bordeaux and loving them, totally laughing

Château Latour-Martillac Blanc, 2005; $39
AOC Pessac-Léognan, Bordeaux, France
Grapes: Sauvignon (55%), Sémillon (44%), Muscadelle (1%)
13% ABV
2,650 cases produced
www.latour-martillac.com
www.bobbofman.com

that there is no market for them here in America. This wine is a steal for the money. I am really proud to include it on the list because these wines are ignored by the media, ignored by the sommeliers, and ignored by customers. Of all the many misconceptions about Bordeaux, the only one that pisses me off more than "they are pricey" is "they are red." In addition to Graves, dry white Bordeaux can be made from Sémillon and Sauvignon Blanc in Pessac-Léognan and Entre-Deux-Mers. And let's not forget that the legendary sweet whites of Sauternes are also part of Bordeaux. Try this wine and you'll never imagine a great glass of Bordeaux the same way again.

Meet the Grape: Sémillon

As the primary white grape in Bordeaux, Sémillon lends its generous body and richness to white blends, acting as a perfect counterpart to the lively acid of Sauvignon Blanc. In addition to its role in dry table wines, Sémillon is a primary variety in the sweet wines of Sauternes. Extensive plantings exist in Chile as well as parts of Australia.

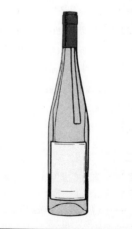

BACKWARD-LOOKING STATEMENT

I'm a young guy, so obviously I have not been around the wine business for as long as some of my seniors. However, I have been drinking and enjoying wine long enough to pine for the good old days. I'm talking about California in the 1990s, and this wine totally takes me back.

From the first sniffy-sniff, this wine just totally blew my socks off with a dark nose of black currants and black raspberry. It's also a bit Grape Ape, with some of that grape Big League Chew. On the palate, the oak has really amazing silkiness, and the secondary flavors are dominated by vegetal celery root, giving the impression of grape juice blended with V8. The finish has hints of cedar box and leather components, like a pair of nice, polished wingtips in your mouth.

The wine also has gorgeous, dry tannins and a great backbone structure that wildly remind me of some of the Spotswood Cabernet and Shafer Hillside Select of the mid-1990s. This wine really struts its pedigree and big balls and is a throwback to an era when Napa Cab was really rocking the place. This is pre-1991 style, before things in Napa started going in a different direction, and I love that it shows a

---

VAYNERCABULARY

Sniffy sniff (n)—*A nasal inhalation executed with the specific purpose of observing flavors in wine. The nose is a far more precise sensory instrument than the mouth, therefore a sniffy sniff is useful as a step in tasting wine.*

Jocelyn Lonen Winery, Napa Valley Cabernet Sauvignon, 2005; $35

Napa Valley, California

Grapes: Cabernet Sauvignon (92%), Cabernet Franc (6%), Malbec (2%)

14.9% ABV

2,700 cases produced

www.jocelynlonen.com

true balance of oak and dark fruit with great, passionate, ripe, explosive berry flavors.

In this wine, the vineyard is speaking to me. So, if like me, you have a real nostalgia for the old-school Caymus and Cakebread, there is no need to dig into your cellar or start hitting the wine auctions, because this wine serves up an almost forgotten era of great Cabernet.

Palate Primer:

Big League Chew

Created by Portland Mavericks pitcher Rob Nelson and New York Yankee All-Star Jim Bouton, Big League Chew is shredded bubble gum packaged in a foil pouch to resemble chewing tobacco. According to Bouton, Nelson made the first gum in a frying pan, and it was rejected by the major candy companies. The product was introduced by Amurol Products in 1980 and sold $18 million in product in its first twelve months. Wm. Wrigley Jr. Company now sells Big League chew in flavors of bubble gum, cotton candy, grape, strawberry, watermelon, sour cherry, and sour apple flavors. www.jimbouton.com

PLEASE HOLD THE OAK

I really hesitate to use the word *hate*. So, I will just say I am not a huge fan of a lot of California Sauvignon Blanc. I've just been disappointed too many times, which is why this crisp, bio-dynamically farmed Sauvignon Blanc is so very refreshing—literally.

On the nose, this wine is very Moscato-esque, very fresh, very vibrant, and simply enjoyable. I get ripe papaya on the nose, which is quite pretty, along with this fizzy peach component. Actually, it's exactly like a Bellini; it's one of those aromas that, when you recognize it, is so specific that it's almost shocking.

The flavor is full of vibrant, clean fruit with a nice citrus blast. This wine has great acidity on the mid-palate, with more peach coming through in the flavor and a long finish. What puts this wine shoulders above many other California Sauvignon Blancs is that it's not trying to be creamy, oaky Chardonnay. Why in God's name do so many West Coast winemakers continue to oak Sauvignon Blanc? It doesn't make sense. It doesn't want the oak. It's like your grand-

---

Palate Primer

Bellini

A Bellini is a classic Italian cocktail that originated in 1948 at Harry's Bar in Venice, Italy. Head bartender Giuseppe Cipriani combined pureed white peaches with the region's sparkling wine, Prosecco, to create this cocktail, a forbear of the mimosa.

**Ceàgo Vinegarden, Sauvignon Blanc,
Kathleen's Vineyard, 2006; $25**

Clear Lake, California
Grape: Sauvignon Blanc
13.5% ABV
4,000 cases produced
www.ceago.com

mother trying to push the borscht on you. And poor Sauvignon Blanc is there helpless, pleading, "Grandma, I don't want any. I don't like it. Really, please, I do not want the damn borscht!" To be fair, this wine has seen some oak. But it was fermented in stainless steel and according to the winemaker, a mere 7 percent of the wine ever saw the inside of a barrel, so it clearly retains all its beautiful acidity and great structure.

Label Lore

The word *ceàgo* is derived from the language of the Pomo Indians, the original inhabitants of the McNab Valley, and translates to "grass seed valley." In keeping with the holistic Native American view of the land, Ceàgo Vinegarden is biodynamically farmed and incorporates habitat breaks in the vineyards.

This wine is exceptional among California Sauvignon Blancs because it speaks of cleanliness, crispness, and freshness, qualities that we more often associate with Loire Valley and New Zealand Sauvignon Blanc. If more California producers would put down the oak chips and shoot for this purity of fruit, we could have a really exciting and impressive assortment of Sauvignon Blanc coming out of California. But for now, this one will do.

 # 64

WHAT'S OLD IS NEW AGAIN

wine country

Before Bordeaux, before Burgundy, there was Douro. Portugal's Douro region, named for the Douro River, which enters from Spain and empties into the Atlantic, is the world's first demarcated wine region, established in 1758. Formerly, most grape production went into Port, but quality red wine production is on the rise.

There's far more to Portugal than just Port. I'm very excited about the Portuguese table wines coming to America, and I believe Douro is the next Napa Valley. It will take some time, but there are so many exciting and impressive wines coming out of this region that the potential is huge. Thankfully, we still have some time to snatch up values like this. I really believe that you could put this wine in a blind tasting against wines from Bordeaux and California, costing as much as $70, and people would be utterly shocked at how well it performs.

With several of the classic Port grape varieties in the mix, this is very much a red-fruit-dominated wine. The aroma is like a cherry reduction sauce with fresh nutmeg, almost like something I want to pour over a breast of duck. On the palate, the overall mouthfeel and structure are really impressive. This wine is clearly made to last, and I think it will endure for seven to ten years easily. It's a very New World–style wine from a very Old World place.

But perhaps the most impressive thing about this wine is how it balances power with great elegance. There is amazing lushness;

Real Companhia Velha, Evel Grande Escolha, 2004; $25
DOC Douro, Portugal
Grapes: Touriga Nacional (50%), Touriga Francesa (25%),
    other grapes (25%)
14% ABV
800 cases imported
www.realcompanhiavelha.pt

extremely firm, rich tannins would make this ideal with a big meal. It's the kind of wine I would pop to impress the boss or a wine-savvy friend, yet it's so beautiful, elegant, and delicious. This wine exudes the kind of poise and polish you'd expect from an Upper East Side socialite. It's been carefully groomed with generations of pedigree. It knows exactly where to place the fork and the spoon.

There are two traditional fortified Ports on this list, and they are great values and offer all the intensity, longevity, and prestige of great Port. But this wine truly represents a revolution for one of the oldest recognized wine regions. It's like the appearance of Peter Fonda in *Easy Rider*. He had the talent of his father and the family resemblance, but was totally relevant for a new generation.

Meet the Grape:
Touriga Nacional

With its low yields and small, concentrated, tannic berries, this grape forms the foundation of nearly every Port wine. Even in small percentages, it provides backbone and durability to these wines and is increasingly important in Portugal's still wines.

#63

A TASMANIAN-ALSATIAN BLEND

This is a wine that, on paper, did not sound all that encouraging. But the second I held it to my nose, I knew I was in for something amazing. I am utterly shocked that this wine smells like $25 to $40 Alsatian wine; really Riesling more than anything else. It absolutely has the bouquet of Alsace. I was expecting Sweet'N Low and candy, and instead this wine delivers dandelion, dried weeds, eggshell—all the things that I adore about Alsace.

On the palate, it comes through with the classic petrol and peach flavors of Riesling, married with the vibrancy and youthful joy of the Southern Hemisphere. This is one of those wines I can really relate to, not just because it's delicious, but because I see myself in this wine. I'm a 31-year-old man, but so many people tell me that I have the glow of a boy. That's what

Label Lore

This wine's name pays homage to Estelle Merle O'Brien Thompson, the original name of screen actress Merle Oberon, who starred in such classic films as *Wuthering Heights* (1939) and *The Dark Angel* (1935), for which she received an Academy Award nomination. Oberon maintained that she was born and raised in St. Helens, a beachside resort on the east coast of Tasmania, Australia. However, it is now widely believed that she was not born in Australia but in Bombay, British India, and concocted the story to make herself more employable.

Pirie South, Estelle, 2006; $17
Tamar Valley, Tasmania, Australia
Grapes: Riesling (50%), Gewürztraminer (30%),
  Pinot Gris (20%)
12.8% ABV
1,200 cases imported
www.pirietasmania.com.au

wine country

The Australian island of Tasmania represents an official wine zone of its own. There are no designated subregions, but there are seven distinct viticultural areas, including the Tamar Valley. Tasmania's cool climate makes it ideal for the production of white wine from Riesling, Chardonnay, Sauvignon Blanc, and Pinot Gris, as well as Pinot Noir and sparkling wine.

this wine really smacks of: It's masculine and sophisticated and true to Alsace, with all the classic grapes and flavors represented, but there is a youthfulness and purity of fruit that make it joyful. As far as food-friendliness, I am downright devastated that I don't have a dozen West Coast Kumamoto oysters right now, because they would be disappearing quickly. Shellfish and seafood—all the things you normally love with Alsace—would just come to life with this wine.

The full-bodied juicy style, along with the big aromatics of Riesling and Gewürztraminer, make this a great way to add some life to a boring chicken breast, or a good choice for white meat turkey. When your mom overcooks the Thanksgiving turkey, yet again, I want you to pop a bottle of this and bring that dried-out bird back to life.

HEARTY AND HEART HEALTHY

Tannat is a grape that is commonly associated with the Madiran region of France. As the name implies, Tannat is tannic. Wines made from Tannat in this part of the world can last for 50 or 100 years. The skins can be so dark, so ripe, so nearly unapproachable that they are probably made for your grandchildren to enjoy. There is really no rushing Tannat. At Cambiata, the wine usually spends two and a half years in the barrel before it's ready to bottle. Then again, people in the Madiran seem to have plenty of time on their hands, since they enjoy one of the world's longest life expectancies, something that has brought scientists like Dr. Roger Corder, author of *The Red Wine Diet*, to the conclusion that Tannat may be the most heart-healthy red wine.

There is no doubt that Tannat is capable of yielding massive red wines. So if that's your style, stop drinking overripe and overmanipulated Cabernet and reach for the

Label Lore

A *cambiata*, in musical language, is a melodic ornamental tone following a principal tone by a skip. It is sometimes called a changed note, and refers also to the added tonal dimension that occurs when two chords momentarily share properties, giving the transition greater depth. The Cambiata brand from Laumann Family Estate Wines includes varietal wines from Tannat and Albariño, two grapes that are relatively uncommon for California.

Cambiata, Estate Bottled Tannat, 2005; $30
Monterey, California
Grape: Tannat
13.9% ABV
375 cases produced
www.cambiatawinery.com

right grape: Tannat. On the nose, I'm smitten by the nutmeg and egg-nog flavors. It has these great classic blackberry and licorice flavors and extraordinary overall polish and elegance. Being from California, this wine is much more approachable than some of the massive French wines from this grape.

Still, the tannins are downright dirty. Dirty, dirty, dirty! It's not fair that something this bitter is surrounded by this kind of fruit. It tastes like a grape picked a little too early, sweet on the outside but the center makes you pucker up faster than eating a Sour Patch Kid. Still, this wine is clearly well made. It's not the classic Tannat, and it might be a little too New World for some, but it is juicy, very solid, and exuberant in its black licorice and blueberry flavors. I think seven to ten years from now it will be toning down a bit.

Palate Primer:

Sour Patch Kids

Created as the penny candy Mars Men in the 1970s, Sour Patch Kids took their new name in the U.S. in 1985. The candy comes in a variety of flavors, including strawberry, grape, apple, and orange, and consists of a soft confectionery center with a granulated sour coating.

LIKE A BEAUTIFUL LAUNDRETTE

We often think of France as a land of wine and cheese, but—incredibly—there is only one region recognized with an AOC for both: Valençay. In addition to a vaguely pyramidal goat cheese, Valençay makes white and red wines out of the usual mishmash of grapes common to this part of the Loire Valley.

This might not be a wine for the New World wine lovers, but it is a great buy for someone a little daring, someone trying to expand their palate, looking to taste something totally new. With a blend of four red grapes (including Pinot Noir, which must really piss off the Burgundy guys), this wine has a distinct nose of detergent. Seriously. It has this classic, sudsy, soapy detergent smell, but with some spicy green components, like a laundromat filled with jalapeño peppers. On the palate there is blackberry fruit, but it's really pretty sour, with a dark, high-cacao chocolate coming through as well. It has a really great mouthfeel, and is incredibly smooth around the edges, with some lilac and violets coming through on the mid-palate, before the nice long exotic finish ending with a mouthful of ripe chocolate-

VAYNERCABULARY

Haunted house (adj)—refers to flavors in a wine that may include cellar and attic aromas, dusty wood, and cobwebs. Much like a Halloween haunted house, these flavors can be somewhat frightening, yet great fun in the right doses.

Clos Delorme, Valençay, 2005; $15

AOC Valençay, Loire Valley, France

Grapes: Gamay (40%), Malbec (30%), Cabernet Franc (20%),
Pinot Noir (10%)

12.5% ABV

500 cases imported

covered-cherry flavors. There is also a little vegetal component coming through on the finish.

In addition, this wine shows a cobweb component. The best way for me to describe it is "haunted house." But there's no reason to be scared off by this odd red blend from an unusual Loire Valley appellation. It is really a wine made for food. If you can't get your hands on some of that strange-shaped local cheese, I think this would be totally intriguing with some venison, game, or lamb stew.

wine country

Valençay is a recently added French AOC wine region, having just received approval for making red and white AOC wines in 2004. They have been making AOC cheese since 1998.

SATELLITE I LOVE

This 30-buck Bordeaux is from a region referred to as one of Bordeaux's satellite districts: Lalande-de-Pomerol. The satellite moniker is slightly deceptive, since the region is actually larger than Pomerol itself. Most important, the wines are less prestigious (read: cheaper), while still offering a taste of authentic Bordeaux.

This wine really reminds me of how great Merlot can be, and how unfortunate it is that one silly movie, however entertaining, can totally blacklist a grape that has made great wine for centuries. There are thousands of Merlots out there; don't let Hollywood tell you what you should and should not drink. Have you noticed that, since *Sideways*, some French Burgundies are actually printing the words "Pinot Noir" on their labels, but none of the great Bordeaux are adding "Merlot"? And suddenly almost every California winery that offers a Pinot Noir has it priced 20 bucks above their other red wines. This is all absurd! These are the same wines they have always been, and the marketers are manipulating you. I've dubbed 2004 the Last of the Mohicans vintage in Bordeaux for good reason, and you should take full advantage of this wine, which has fallen into the cracks between the great 2005 and very good 2003 vintage. Unlike those wines, which are being snatched up, this vintage should be on shelves and available for a few years to come.

On the palate, this red has huge polish and extreme length. What I

Château La Fleur de Boüard, 2004; $30

AOC Lalande-de-Pomerol, Bordeaux, France

Grapes: Merlot (80%), Cabernet Franc (15%),
   Cabernet Sauvignon (5%)

13.5% ABV

4,000–6,000 cases produced

www.lafleurdebouard.com

www.bobbofman.com

Meet the Grape: Merlot

The most widely planted grape in Bordeaux, Merlot is a supporting grape throughout the region, except in the right bank wines of St-Émilion and Pomerol, where it is the primary variety. Merlot shares many flavor characteristics with Cabernet Sauvignon, but often shows greener flavors and softer tannins, which allow it to mature earlier. Merlot can ripen in slightly cooler climates than Cabernet Sauvignon and has proliferated throughout the winemaking world.

really love, in addition to all the smokiness, blueberries, and blackberries, is that it possesses great density, silkiness, and posture. I really like to personify wine and consider its posture. This wine is a well-trained dog, or a really well-behaved child. It is happy, not suppressed, with stature and confidence and joie de vivre. It is really one of the more polished 2004 Bordeaux I have come across, with a freshness of fruit, trueness of flavor, and refreshing lack of manipulation. This is textbook Bordeaux at a very fair price. If you have seen the 2005 prices and are concerned about ever getting your first taste of true Bordeaux, here is your chance. Get out your phone and text the name of this wine to yourself right now. Carry it with you like a string around your finger, and when you finally taste this, you'll know what Bordeaux is all about.

PORT FOR THE IMPATIENT

When the traffic light turns green, do you utilize your prize-fighter reflexes to hit the horn if traffic does not move *immediately*? And when you get bumped into corporate voice mail, do you start tapping zero hoping to get a receptionist? If so, you are not a person who should be cellaring wine. Fortunately, I have the wine for you.

This Port is a great counterpart to the other Port in this book, because it's ready to drink now. Yes, right now! And it's out there, in the market, and probably priced under $100 almost everywhere. It's actually not a bad premium for a pre-aged wine, considering you didn't need to schlep it around between three apartments and two houses and keep your mitts off of it for two decades.

The year 1983 was a good solid vintage, and according to Warre's, one of their best—but it gets lost in the shuffle between 1977 and 1985. That means that this wine brings enormous value in a package that is drinkable and approachable right now. This Port has beautiful

Palate Primer:

Butterscotch

Made by boiling sugar, butter, cream, and vanilla, butterscotch is a confection similar to toffee, but usually not as hard. The first usage of the word was recorded in Doncaster, England, where Samuel Parkinson began making the candy in 1817.

Warre's & Co., Vintage Port, 1983; $80
Oporto, Portugal
Grapes: Touriga Nacional, Touriga Francesa, Tinta Barroca,
    Tinta Roriz
20% ABV
12,000 cases produced
www.warre.com

hazelnut-butterscotch aromas, along with rich blackberry and per-fume components. I feel like I am eating blackberries while strolling through the Bergdorf's fragrance department, and all those women keep hounding me to take their little cards and fragrance samples . . . but hey, I'm eating blackberries here.

The gorgeous tannins of this wine know just how to caress my palate, and it is incredibly rich, juicy, and silky-smooth. The perfect time for this Port would be when you're out for dinner with your boss and someone starts passing around the box of Montecristos, which you dread because big, fat cigars are not for impatient people. Scan the dessert wine list for the Warre's 1983 and tell your boss what I just told you. People are going to absolutely adore this wine—with a cigar or a dessert—and you will be a star for recommending it. So sit back, light your stogie, and relax with a glass or two. This Port has been waiting around for over twenty-five years. What's the rush?

IT'S IN THE MAIL

L
ike it or not, some of the best wines in California never make it to your local wine store. This wine, for instance, may be one of the best California Chardonnays I've ever tasted, and it, like all the wines of Ambullneo, is made in small numbers and sold directly through the winery's mailing list. Then again, considering this compares to some of the $400 Montrachets I've had the pleasure to taste, this is one mail offer that does not belong on the pile with the bills and the Land's End catalog.

This white is loaded with complexity, and the aroma offers all the things that really turn me on about Chardonnay: amazing, green grass; watermelon peel; ripe pears; and little hints of oak. The flavor is ripping with pear, some gorgeous cedar, and a little smack from Hacksaw Jim Duggan's wood plank. There is beautiful acidic balance, and golden, silky elegance on the back end. The finish is a scrap bin of fruit, with apple core, melon peel, and papaya pulp. It's also worth mentioning that Ambullneo is a cuvée specialist, so this wine, Big Paw, is not a single vineyard

Label Lore

The Ambullneo is a dog breed created by Mark Reasinger, PhD, by crossing various European mastiffs with several types of bulldogs. This powerful and protective breed is 57.5 percent mastiff and 42.5 percent bulldog, and the acronym Ambullneo is derived from the terms American, Bull Breeds, and Neapolitan Mastiff.

Ambullneo Vineyards, Big Paw Chardonnay, 2006; $60
Santa Maria Valley, California
Grape: Chardonnay
13.4% ABV
340 cases produced
www.ambullneovineyards.com

wine, but a product of their skilled blending. Man, this finish is going on for days.

This is the type of wine that made Chardonnay America's sweetheart. This is from more innocent times, before the oak monster got hold of this beauty and dragged her off to the trailer park. The flavor is explosive, rich, and everything you could ever dream of in a Chardonnay, with incredible purity and balance to the fruit. This effort is shockingly good and will last five to seven years in the cellar, for sure. If you're looking to drink some life-changing Chardonnay, sometimes you have to go direct to the source.

Palate Primer:

Cedar

The product of a coniferous tree, cedar wood is a desirable flavor in wine and is most common in red wines, especially Cabernet Sauvignon and Rhône red varieties. The smell is often described as cigar box or cedar box, since cedar wood is used in these applications for its humidity-maintaining characteristics. The flavor of cedar may arise as the result of a wine's grape, aging, or *terroir*.

SUSPEND YOUR DISBELIEF

If you watch a great movie, or even a reality TV show, and constantly remind yourself that it has all been contrived and edited and calculated, you're going to miss a lot of enjoyment. Sometimes with wine, it helps to take the same approach.

Philippe Melka has a hand in this wine made by the people at Ferrari Carano, and I'd be remiss to not include one of his efforts. Philippe is a producer of hedonistic fruit bomb cult wines. However, Melka manages to bring an Old World flair to his wines, and I think he achieves more balance than many of the competing winemakers out there.

The color of this wine is just gorgeous. The nose offers a good solid shot of vanilla and cherry and oak—classic Cabernet flavors. There is also cedar box and blackberries, not the blackberries you buy in the store, but the ones I eat while I'm out playing paintball—which are fundamentally different. This wine has paintball blackberries! It really is a bit of a throwback and reminds me of the 1991 and 1994 vintage California Cabs. In recent years, a lot of wines have gotten a

VAYNERCABULARY

Fruit bomb (n)—*A wine in which an abundance of fruit is the primary flavor, often at the expense of additional complexity. Many New World wines are identified as fruit bombs, which may be positive—or not—depending on the drinker's preferences.*

PreVail Mountain Winery, West Face, 2004; $47

Alexander Valley, California
Grapes: Cabernet Sauvignon (70%), Syrah (30%)
14.9% ABV
3,000 cases produced
www.prevailwines.com

little extreme with their oak, alcohol, and ripeness. They remind me of some of the cars we drive in America—big to the point of absurdity. It's time to take a step back, and I am seeing a slow return to more classic-style wines, both at Wine Library and on my own palate. So this wine, while it is somewhat manipulated, is a real step in the right direction.

Now to give it a whirl: Aaaaaaaaaaaaaahhh. Yes, the oak monster is here. However, if Larry Bird and Magic Johnson can become friends, if Bill Russell and Wilt Chamberlain can become friends, if Sugar Ray Leonard and Thomas Hearns can be buddies, then the oak monster and I can put aside our differences, hold hands, and enjoy this wine together. The oak complexity here is really beautiful, especially with this fruit-filling quality that serves up massive fruit.

This is a big and bold wine, a lunch meeting wine, where power is the point, and everything being said is a little bit fake anyway. That's where you want to pour this blend. I am going to let myself be tricked and enjoy this wine because, like watching *Life of Ryan* or *Gossip Girl*, it's oh so good.

#56

A BOOK BY ITS COVER

wine country

Paso Robles—literally "the pass of the oaks"—includes more than 170 wineries and 26,000 acres of vineyard. With a variety of microclimates and soils, warm days and cool nights, more than forty varieties of wine grapes are cultivated here. www.pasowine.com

I yell at people all the time for buying wine based on its label. But honestly, I am in love with this wine label. It's cream-colored. Man, I love cream labels. There is this foil-stamped tree and an owl. The font's right. Hey—I am just *really* into this.

Back to the wine. The smell of this wine is a little manipulated, something I don't normally subscribe to. But in this case, I don't really give a rat's ass for one simple reason: It's delicious. Sometimes your team gives up thirteen runs in the first inning. Sometimes you are going to cancel your dinner reservation and order pizza. Sometimes you just don't want to think too hard. You just want to say screw it and enjoy the moment. That's the time for this wine.

This wine has a lot stacked against it. At 16 bones, it's not inexpensive. Also, it's Merlot, which makes it a target for getting pissed on. Yet, this has some really nice dark chocolate and chalkboard on the nose that I really enjoy. I had Mrs. Long for sophomore English. She was totally rad, and my move was to get there five minutes before her and pound all the erasers against the chalkboard to create an enormous cloud of distraction and chalk dust in the air. I can smell

Paso Creek, Merlot, 2005; $16
Paso Robles, California
Grapes: Merlot
13.5% ABV
30,000 cases produced

that moment in this wine—dark fruit, chalk dust, and a little hint of green asparagus.

In the flavor, I really enjoy the Cherry Coke component, and the tannins are firm and fair, like that boxing referee Joe Cortez, who always says "I'm fair but firm." These tannins swiped his catchphrase. Then there is the referee Mills Lane, who used the catch phrase "Let's get it on!" and nailed Tyson for trying to eat an ear and became a TV judge. He has nothing to do with these tannins.

With Wine Library TV, I am all about winning people over to new things, whether it is Albariño or loud-mouthed Jersey kids. I want people to step outside their comfort zone. This wine is manipulated, a bit of a science project, but it still works for me. I can taste that it is fake, but the overall easiness, fun, and tastiness of this wine still totally rock. So kudos to Paso Creek for making a good wine with a great label.

THE EXCEPTION TO THE RULE

Back in 1395, Philippe the Bold was hating on the Gamay grape so much that he banned it from Burgundy. If it were up to me, Governor Schwarzenegger would do the same thing to Sauvignon Blanc in California. I have not made any secret of my disdain for California Sauvignon Blanc. It's just that there are so many grapes that have more potential there, *and* there are so many areas of the world, like the Loire Valley, New Zealand, and Chile, that totally spank California when it comes to Sauvignon Blanc. Why bother?

The frightening thing about wine, however, is that just when you think you have it all figured out, along comes something to shatter your conceptions. I am in love with this Napa Valley Sauvignon Blanc for its celery root meets fresh-cut, dew-covered grass and pink grapefruit aromas that echo some of the New Zealand Sauvignon Blanc out there. It has a similarly aromatic, refreshing nose, too.

The flavors are extremely fresh with a blend of basil, oregano, and

Palate Primer:

7UP

7UP was created as Bib-Label Lithiated Lemon-Lime Soda by Charles Leiper Grigg in 1929. The origin of the 7UP name is disputed, but it is not the pH of the beverage as some suggest. Diet 7UP has a pH of 3.67, less acidic than pure lemon juice at 2.3. www.7up.com

Alpha Omega, Sauvignon Blanc, 2007; $34
Napa Valley, California
Grape: Sauvignon Blanc
14.1% ABV
5,500 cases produced
www.aowinery.com

lemongrass on the palate. It's almost spritzy, with a 7UP character and this spectacularly sharp acidity that cuts like a razor blade. This stuff is so sharp that it will slice through any fishy-fish like a fillet knife, so you need to try that pairing.

The only place where this wine lacks is in QPR (quality to price ratio). If this wine came from anywhere else for 34 bones, I could not see it on this list. It's simply overpriced for the category. So, I'm serving this wine with a chaser of irony and a side of humble pie. Does it deserve to be on my list of wines with thunder? Yes! Because this wine has proved me wrong. It shows there is always an exception to the rule, and even after tasting thousands of California Sauvignon Blancs I really did not like, that is no reason to give up. There are no absolutes in wine.

This is a groundbreaking effort, and if the Governator ever decrees we tear up all the Sauvignon Blanc in California, I'll personally sign the petition to let Alpha Omega keep their vines.

#54   GO SOUTH, VALUE HUNTERS

Sometimes you have to look outside the obvious wine-growing regions to turn up good values. If you're up for turning a few stones, Minervois is a good place to start, because this Languedoc region is mostly hot, rugged, rocky terrain. However, it's worth the effort. Were this wine packaged in a bottle that said Rhône or Barossa on it, rather than some cryptic appellation from the south of France, I would easily expect to pay $50 for it. This is exactly the sort of wine I'm searching for.

Château Maris is one of the primary labels for Comte Cathare, which includes several small bio-dynamic properties in France owned by Englishman Bertie Eden. Not only does Comte Cathare grow grapes biodynamically, but they produce two specially labeled wines that provide funding for the Rainforest Foundation UK and for the preservation of ancient trees through the Woodland Trust. These guys are not just hugging the trees, they are actually saving them, and you have to love winemakers who love the soil.

Label Lore

"Certified Biodynamic" wine is made from grapes that are grown using a series of principles created by Austrian philosopher-scientist Rudolf Steiner in 1924. Biodynamic farming views the farm in respect to cosmic rhythms and requires the application of soil treatments made from, among other things, quartz, cow horn, and stag bladder.

Château Maris, La Touge Syrah, 2004; $23

AOC Minervois La Livinière, Languedoc-Roussillon, France
Grape: Syrah
14.5% ABV
4,500 cases produced
www.comtecathare.com

This wine has really beautiful ripe strawberry coming through on the nose, along with this incredibly nice Asian spice element. It's actually very Asian, almost reminding me of soy sauce. There is also an intriguing charcoal, smoky-barbecue aspect, almost like a grill loaded with sizzling smoked ribs.

On the palate, a massively interesting sour cherry component is coming through, along with these really ripe, pleasant fruits on the mid-palate, followed by very firm, ripe tannins. This wine is just a gorgeous expression of pure Syrah fruit. It's not over-oaked; it's not trying to be something else; it is just oozing with integrity. This wine has three to four years of aging ability in it. It may not be the first place to look for familiar, easy-to-pronounce names, but in the south of France, value rules the day.

wine country

Recognized in 1999, La Livinière is the first and only cru in Minervois. In order to produce exemplary wines, the cru focuses on the region's best grapes. Syrah and Mourvèdre must account for a minimum of 40 percent of the blend. The combination of Syrah and Grenache must account for 60 percent. And Carignan and Cinsault must account for no more than 40 percent. Confusing as hell, but it seems to be working.

SWEET THING

Let me warn you: This sparkling wine is a little sweet. Honestly, it's flat-out sweet, which is not totally surprising, considering Moscatel grapes are often used for making raisins in California and are served as dessert in Spain. It almost reminds me of something out of the 1980s, something your parents sipped while chilling to Linda Ronstadt—but hey, that's my era too. Most important, this wine makes a statement that I want to share: Sweet wine does not have to taste like crap.

I'd love to see all the people who enjoy these lightly sweet sparklers put down the Asti Spumante and Moscato d'Asti and try this flavorful, aromatic, and yes—sweet—wine. It is *way* superior to almost all of those other wines. The nose has an ice-pop component, almost like a cup of lemon Italian ice, and I just love those things. It has clear-cut sweetness coming through, somewhat honeyesque with juicy, ripe cantaloupe.

On the palate, there is a hint of dryness on the initial attack, enough to really tease your tastebuds, but then in comes all that melon and cantaloupe sweetness. This wine may not change your

---

VAYNERCABULARY

-esque (adj)—*a suffix indicating a notable resemblance to a distinctive character. While not entirely plastic, a wine's aroma might be described as plasticesque, candyesque, tea-esque, honeyesque.*

life, but it is a little bit unusual, does a great job of representing for its grape, and is just a lot of fun. Whether you're hanging out on the porch or looking for something fizzy for the holidays, I think this wine will find a lot of fans. It would also work to cleanse the palate and cut the heat on some spicy takeout, like Thai with Panang curry or good old General Tso's chicken. I'd also enjoy this wine with some bleu cheese preparations, much the way Sauternes's sweetness couples with funky cheeses, but with a much lighter body and frothy texture. You know they always say American wine drinkers ask for dry but want sweet. So be true to your taste. Come and get a little sugar from Gary.

Meet the Grape:
Moscatel

Also known as Muscat of Alexandria, Moscatel is just one member of the aromatic Muscat family of grapes. It has the highest sugar content, and in addition to being made into wine, it is consumed as table grapes or dried for raisins. This particular Muscat is found across Spain and is a staple variety in the DOs of Málaga and Valencia.

PAINTING THE TOWN PURPLE

If you've ever wondered what purple paint tastes like, this is it. Or, at least, it's the way I always imagined, as a little kid, purple paint might taste.

I know almost no one goes into a wine shop looking to buy Hungarian wines, so this is another case of how the wine world is changing—in a really positive way. This wine is fascinating stuff from so many angles. The aroma is very flower-driven, with these classic dark, dried rose petals. It's got some of that cheap Dollar Store potpourri, along with a hint of blueberry jam, but these are some badass flowers—they really bully the fruit and dominate the nose.

In the flavor, there is that purple paint, almost a fantasy flavor I know, but that's the image I get because it's not heavy or intense; just a medium-bodied, very clean, very fun, bright flavor. There is also a hint of Grape Big League Chew, but don't misunderstand me—this is not some New World fruit bomb. It has really great backbone and sourness to it. It is so fresh, clean, and vibrant that I could see a lot of Pinot Noir fans getting pumped about this wine. There is also a vegetal broccoli and asparagus component

Label Lore

This wine takes the moniker Noir Gold for its dark red, nearly black color. It's this deep, inky color that earned the wines of Szekszárd, in the south of Hungary, and Eger, south-west of Tokaj, their traditional name—Bull's Blood.

Takler Noir Gold Kékfrankos Reserve, 2006; $30
Szekszárd, Hungary
Grapes: Kékfrankos
14.5% ABV
600 cases imported
www.takler.com

to the flavor along with some earthiness, like soil. It's not damp, leafy forest floor soil, however; this is the stuff you buy in a bag at the Home Depot. This wine is just really interesting stuff with a nice long finish, and I could see this being friendly with a lot of foods. Above all, I'm thinking quail, hen, all those little birds. (Little bird lovers, please don't come after me.)

If I had to compare this to another wine, I would say it is Barossa Valley Shiraz meets traditional Volnay from Burgundy. You blend those together and let it mellow a bit, and this is what you get. Of course, it would be much easier—and cheaper—to pick up this Hungarian beauty. This may not be for everyone, but I know there are a few palates out there that are going to love this, so I have to tell you to take a chance on the color purple.

Meet the Grape:
Kékfrankos

Also known as Blaufränkisch in Austria, Limberger in Germany, and Lemberger in Washington State, this red grape is light in tannin and high in acidity. It often draws comparison to Beaujolais' Gamay, and is sometimes referred to as Gamé in Hungary, where it is a leading red variety in Szekszárd and Eger.

GO SEE A SPECIALIST

There's absolutely nothing wrong with a winery making a large portfolio of wines. This book includes several wines from large *négociants* like Domaine Louis Jadot, and New World producers like Montevina Winery, each of which makes literally dozens of wines. But I also want to emphasize that it's okay to do one thing really well. Señorío San Vicente is one winery, with one vineyard, growing one grape, to make one wine. It sounds simple, but this sort of approach leaves no room for error, which only makes me more amazed at the consistent thunder these guys bring.

I've been enjoying the wine for at least ten vintages now, and I can honestly say this is the brightest, most expressive San Vincente I've ever tasted. This wine has a very interesting nose. It almost reminds me of putting blueberries into a tire with this rubbery tire component that I actually find elegant. It is very polished and very creamy on the nose, with a nice, subtle hint of vanilla. There is also some licorice and an overall hedonistic impression to the nose. The aromas are a little tight, but I'm drinking this wine very, very young, and

VAYNERCABULARY

Terroir (n)—*pronounced ter-WAH, a French term for the impact of site on wine grapes and the resulting wine. "Terroir" refers to the cumulative effect of soil, climate, weather, and other terrestrial factors and the influence they have on wine, with an almost mystical implication. The entire French AOC system revolves around the importance of terroir.*

Señorío San Vicente, San Vicente, 2005; $57
DOC Rioja, Spain
Grape: Tempranillo Peludo
14.5% ABV
1,000 cases imported
www.eguren.com

judging by my past experience, I think over the next two to three years it is really going to open up

From the first sip, the polish of this wine dumbfounds me. It is very full-bodied, very viscous, almost like the texture of nail polish—not that I should know what nail polish tastes like. It really shows great elegance, with rich blueberry jam flavors that remind me of the blueberry pancake topping at IHOP. There is really nice cassis fruit, and great *terroir*—which is a fancy way of saying dirt. This is a bright and exciting and beautiful wine. So many Spanish wines jump right into the deep end. They are almost too explosive, too over-the-top. But San Vicente is the type of Rioja that a Bordeaux drinker could come to love. Perhaps best of all, it's widely available and not too expensive. Being a multitalented winery demands respect, but it can also pay to specialize.

THINK INSIDE THE BOX

I did not select this wine because it's in a box, but despite the fact that it's in a box (more correctly called a bag-in-box). The bottom line: this all-Merlot Bordeaux is of great quality, and by offering this wine in a box format the producer has actually managed to launch the QPR (quality to price ratio) to the stratosphere, which you know we love. At $28, this three-liter box of wine, equal to four standard wine bottles, amounts to only $7 per bottle. Personally, I think this wine outshines many California Merlots in the $13 to $15 range.

I look forward to a day when whether wine comes in a bottle, or a box, or a tin can, or a Mason jar is not even a topic of conversation. If the wine is good, I personally don't care. And I embrace this wine for its quality. Period. However, there is a stigma about box wine in the U.S. that bears addressing. Because of box wine like Franzia and the fact that box wines are found under the bed in most college dorm rooms, everyone thinks all box wine is crap. However, in Australia

Palate Primer:

Nesquik

Known simply as Nestlé Quik for generations in the United States, the name of this popular chocolate powder for flavoring milk became Nesquik in 1999. Nestlé changed the formula of Nesquik powder last year, reducing the amount of sugar by 33 percent.

Clos des Moiselles, Le Bordeaux Merlot, 2005; $28/3 liters
AOC Bordeaux, France
Grape: Merlot
13% ABV
6,000 cases imported
www.closdesmoiselles.com

and much of Europe, premium wine in boxes is quite common.

On the nose, this wine has a beautiful dark cherry mixed with cocoa, sort of like a Nestlé Nesquik powder, which I am really enjoying. In the flavor, there are highly focused dark cherry flavors, with hints of both vanilla and mocha on the finish, and in a Starbucks era, I think these flavors are going to appeal to a lot of people. But I don't want to imply that this Merlot has no guts; there are some serious tannins here, extremely structured and polished, along with a little broccoli vegetal action.

With its easy-drinking style and convenient package, I consider this the ultimate walk-by wine. You're walking by on your way from the kitchen to the TV, or to check on the kids, to the office—or whatever it is you do—and this shiny silver box on the counter is screaming, "Drink me!" I don't care if it's 9 a.m. That urge, combined with this package and this wine, is absolutely nothing to be embarrassed about. You can grab a half of a glass and you're on your way. I really have to give kudos to winemaker Oswaldo Hernandez for such a fine effort and such a progressive package. According to him, this package will last for two months after opening in the refrigerator. However, I believe once you have a taste of this Merlot, that won't even be an option.

ASZÚ! GOD BLESS YOU

Dessert wines are a huge challenge for wine critics. Look at Robert M. Parker Jr. or *Wine Spectator* and you'll see *all* these dessert wines with scores of 94, 95, 96, even many from Australia. The bottom line: We are human and we love sugar. These wines are so over-the-top with sugar, you throw a few into your daily wine tasting and suddenly it's like going to Mardi Gras instead of happy hour, like the fifty-yard line at the Super Bowl instead of Monday night on the couch. You're only human. You can't help but love the sugary fruit that dessert wine delivers.

To select the handful of dessert wines included in this list, I try to look beyond the sugar for complexity, flavor, balance, and value. For me, that often means Tokaji. If you go back 70 or 80 years, Tokaji was a heck of a lot more important—and interesting—to the wine world than Bordeaux. These are simply amazing dessert wines that pleasantly surprise nearly everyone who experiences them. And, their low profile makes these wines a great value. The "Aszú" in Tokaji Aszú

Label Lore

The proportion of Aszú grapes added to a dry base wine to create sweet Tokaji Aszú is traditionally measured in "puttonyos." The number of puttonyos in an Aszú wine is indicated on the label with a number from 3 to 6. This number now reflects the precise sugar content of the wine, from 3 puttonyos (60g/l) to 6 puttonyos (150g/l).

Domaine Imperial Hétszölö, Tokaji Aszú 5 Puttonyos, 2001; $45/500 ml
Primae Classes, Tokaj, Hungary
Grapes: Furmint (65%), Hàrslevelü (33%), Muscat (2%)
11.5% ABV
1,500 cases imported
www.barriere-freres.com
www.bobbofman.com

refers to grapes that have been affected by *Botrytis cinerea*, also known as noble rot. This fungus consumes water from the grapes, concentrating the sugars and flavors for this legendary sweet wine.

The aroma of this wine is like a creation from a pastry chef in a five-star French restaurant. There is a little of the requisite cheap brandy, along with gobs of brown sugar, peaches, butterscotch, and dried apricots. A little whipped cream on the side and a drizzle of fruit sauce on the plate, and you have this wine.

Even on the palate, it is amazing how much it resembles a lavish dessert, with its deluge of caramel and apricot and peach juice. But like a great dessert, it is never too sugary, with a superb balance thanks to some great acidity. This is a fairly premium Tokaji at a very fair price. Next time you need a sweet treat, I urge you to look to this wine—and to Hungary—because dollar for dollar, they make the best dessert wines in the world.

NO RESERVATIONS ABOUT RAO'S

New York foodies like me will know Rao's as one of the most legendary and tightly booked restaurants in Manhattan. The wait to get a taste of the critically acclaimed Neapolitan cuisine at this ten-seat Harlem restaurant is often a year or more. But you can go out and grab a bottle of their eponymous Prosecco any day of the week.

I'm thrilled to be able to include another sparkling wine in this list. With seven examples, sparkling wine might seem heavily represented in my 101 wines, but I think the category includes some of the most exciting efforts and amazing values in the wine world. And don't make the mistake of thinking all sparkling wines are the same: Bubbly wines come in a great variety of grapes, sweetness, effervescence, quality, and price, which makes them every bit as diverse as the still wines on this list.

I'm a huge personal fan of these wines for their refreshing, food-friendly qualities, and I embrace the opportunity to send corks popping and foster a greater appreciation for sparklers in the U.S.

The nose of this wine offers an enormous blast of Crystal Light powder, filled with lemonade and fresh fruit. Linda Evans would be totally pumped to drink this wine! Forget *Dynasty*—that cougar single-handedly built the Crystal Light brand. The nose finishes very fresh and very clean, with a little spritz of lime.

On the palate, this wine is loaded with great acidity, lemon and

Rao's, Prosecco VSAQ Extra Dry, NV; $15
IGT Prosecco, Italy
Grape: Prosecco
11% ABV
20,000 cases produced
www.raoswines.com

lime, and a fresh-baked bread component. There is also some nice fig flavor on the finish. With its bright acidity and great fizz, it's easy to see why Prosecco excites so many people. This example is clean, crisp, and affordable, in other words—exactly what I look for in a summertime drink or a brunch buddy. Next time you're hanging on the porch, screw the overpriced Snapple and pop a bottle of this Prosecco. I would also really enjoy this with raw oysters or any type of shellfish. While I am not a regular at the Rao's in New York or the second location in Las Vegas, if the food is as good as this Prosecco, they can book me for two at 8:00 this Friday. Please.

Meet the Grape:
Prosecco

The Prosecco grape lends its name to both the Italian DOC region north of Venice and the sparkling wine it produces. The grapes of Prosecco are large, loosely packed, and golden yellow in color. By law, a minimum of 85 percent of the Italian sparkling wine Prosecco must come from the Prosecco grape variety. www.prosecco.it

SHRIVEL UP AND DRY

When I taste this wine, I feel like the California Raisins characters from my childhood sang "I Heard It Through the Grapevine" one too many times and someone slaughtered them and buried them in my mouth. The reason for the profound, delicious, and macabre image of this raisin massacre is simple: Amarone is made entirely from dried grapes. In order to make this wine, Campagnola first harvests the grapes, then air-dries them in a carefully controlled environment for ninety days, during which they lose more than 35 percent of their weight. Raisined grapes are responsible for several wonderful wines of the Veneto, most notably Amarone, but some also find their way into the more basic Valpolicella and Recioto wines.

The aroma of this wine actually reminds me of going into Patel's Cash and Carry in Iselin, New Jersey. There is this pervasive Far Eastern Indian spice on the nose. I don't know what spices they combine to get that beautiful flavor, but they are all in here. Mixed with the spice is this very clever chocolate aroma. In addition to the

Palate Primer:

Raisinets

Introduced in 1927 by the Blumenthal Chocolate Company, Raisinets consist of California raisins covered in milk chocolate. Nestlé acquired the popular movie concession brand in 1984. www.nestleclassics.com

wine country

The Veneto region in the north of Italy is home to the city of Venice and more DOC wine than any other Italian region, including red, white, and sparkling wines. In addition to Amarone and Valpolicella, Veneto is home to Bardolino, Soave, and the sparkling wine Prosecco.

dominant raisin flavor on the palate, there is also a little hint of prunes along with milk chocolate, almost like Raisinets candy, and on the finish some sourdough bread crust.

I think wines like this, although big in style, full-bodied, and high in alcohol, have the potential to convert non–red wine drinkers. The fruit in here is so dense and so profound that it gives a sense of sweetness that I think could persuade a lot of people who are struggling with red wine to join the party. Like most Amarone, this wine will handle five to ten years of cellaring with ease. But if you choose to drink it now, I'm suggesting you do so right after placing your order for a plate of gnocchi with Parmesan.

SMELLS LIKE POOP

Pardon the mild profanity, but there is no other way to describe the aroma of this wine. And, after all, I do mean it in the best possible way. The nose of this wine is somewhat awkward, with an enormous amount of ostrich poop, lamb poop—not your typical Burgundy cow and horse poop, but other farm animal manure. (Don't ask me how I know the difference.) There is a little sulphur in here too. Overall, this nose is funk, funk, funky! I think a lot of people might be taken aback by this, so if you don't like a lot of poo in your wine, consider this a warning.

In the flavor, the goji berry fruit is mixed with your favorite smoky barbecue and bacon and Canadian ham is just totally blistering my palate. The mid-palate structure is really beautiful, soft with gorgeous tannins. And the finish is like cranberry cream sauce. Imagine making cranberry and sour cream sauce, then slathering it all over a pile of fried bacon or a smoked rib. Sounds good, right? That is exactly what this tastes like. This Pinot is gorgeous, complex, and

Palate Primer:
Poop
In reference to animal manure, which comes from *manuren*, meaning "to cultivate land," poop is a valuable nitrogen-rich fertilizer comprised of the excreted food and straw bedding of domestic animals. The poop of herbivores is milder than that of carnivores, but should still be considered inedible.

Lachini Vineyards, Estate Pinot Noir, 2005; $45
Willamette Valley, Oregon
Grape: Pinot Noir
14.5% ABV
1,140 cases produced
www.lachinivineyards.com

worldly in its approach. It does something that Oregon achieves really well: starting off New World in the initial attack, but turning Burgundian on the finish. This wine also has some burnt tire aromas. Remember when you were a kid and you would have a skidding contest on your BMX bike to see who could lay the longest skid mark on the street? That smell is in here.

With its total funkiness and Old World attitude, I can imagine serious Pinot Noir drinkers loving this. If you came to Pinot post-*Sideways*, post the ripeness epidemic and Petite Sirah infusion, this is not the wine for you. But if you are a longtime Pinot fan, I think you will adore this.

This is a wine that will drink great over the next four to six years and reminds me why Oregon is *the* place to plant Pinot Noir in America. Right now, I just want to forget all the work I have to do, kick back with this wine and a plate heaping with whipped mashed potatoes and lamb shank, and watch some *Facts of Life* reruns. This is that sort of comforting, contemplative wine.

A BOUNTY OF BORDEAUX

#45

I f it seems like there is a crapload of Bordeaux on this list, there is. It's not that I love Bordeaux above other regions, but in looking at the most exciting wines of the year, I need to chase the thunder and follow the value. And right now, that means Bordeaux, class of 2005, baby!

The weather for the 2005 vintage was so ideal that the quality is showing up everywhere. Not to take anything away from these winemakers, but picture me pointing at you as you read this: You, yes you, could have made a great 2005 Bordeaux. The vintage was that perfect, rivaling 1961 and 1982. All the experts were hyping this vintage, and I don't usually buy all that crap, but in this case, all it took was one taste and I was convinced. What is so cool about coming across a vintage like this, one that most of us see only a few times in our wine-drinking careers, is that Bordeaux 2005 is something that I am going to carry with me forever.

Saint-Émilion is fascinating, because as a more approachable, Merlot-dominated wine, it really captured the attention of casual wine drinkers in the 1990s. It brought Bordeaux to people who were not strictly Bordeaux enthusiasts. And this estate captures every-

Label Lore

Château Barde-Haut is owned by the Gracin-Cathiard family, operators of three wine estates, another of which appears on this list at number 36: Château Haut-Bergey, 2005

Château Barde-Haut, 2005; $43
AOC Saint-Émilion Grand Cru, Bordeaux, France
Grapes: Merlot (85%), Cabernet Franc (15%)
14.5% ABV
3,300 cases produced
www.vignoblesgarcin.com
www.bobbofman.com

thing I love about Saint-Émilion at a really great price. And, the estate is located right next to Troplong-Mondot, one of the great, if not the greatest, Saint-Émilion producers.

This wine is so licoricey and spicy, it really makes me think of the Orient. With its potent black tea, hints of licorice, and a whole spice rack of exotic notes, I call this the Asian Bordeaux. It has pretty, pure plum. Is that P cubed? I like that. This wine and this vintage mean something personal to me. I can almost guarantee that in the coming years, I will have far fewer Bordeaux that I am excited about recommending and sharing, so let's just enjoy the ride together. This vintage is that special!

Meet the Grape:
Cabernet Franc

With less pigment and less tannin than Cabernet Sauvignon, Cab Franc has long been useful as a blending grape on both banks of Bordeaux. France's Loire Valley, where the grape is known as Breton, is one of the few places where Cab Franc plays the primary role. In the New World, Cabernet Franc has found a home in cooler regions like New York's Long Island.

STORE-BRAND OPUS ONE

For all of those people who have relished Joseph Phelps Insignia in the past and now realize that it has become way too expensive and clearly overpriced for what it is, this wine is for you.

This mostly Cabernet blend is gorgeous, dark ruby-red in color. And the first thing that comes to mind when I take a sniffy-sniff is a sugar cube in a glass of V8 juice. There is a watermelon-meets-strawberry blended drink aroma. Surely someone has blended those two together. It seems everything has been blended. Pretty soon, instead of Chablis, we'll be able to stop by the 7-Eleven for a lemon and rock Slurpee. Anyway, what is unbelievable and so beautiful to me is this precise tomato component on the tail end of the nose.

On the palate, this wine has got enormous structure and an almost dairy component on the finish. It has some of that classic vanilla oak that tells me the oak monster is about to make his appearance (*insert oak monster sound effect*). I am scared crapless of the oak monster, but I think this time he comes in peace. So, I'm going to enjoy his company, maybe play a little pinochle. The fruit on this wine is just massive—a hedonistic fruit bomb that is so powerful, so rich, so structured, and a complete brouhaha of chaos—yet I don't hate it at all.

Like me, this wine had a guiding hand. And much the way my mom set down good boundaries to control my over-the-top, extro-

Alpha Omega, Proprietary Red Wine, 2005; $68
Napa Valley, California
Grapes: Cabernet Sauvignon (69%), Merlot (31%)
14.7% ABV
1,400 cases made
www.aowinery.com

verted personality, these winemakers have been able to coddle and comfort and nurture this fruit. I really credit them for crafting such a charismatic and loving bottle of wine. If this were easy, everyone would be doing it. What they have managed to do is to take this huge fruit and, without totally caging the animal, walk it around the yard and teach it some boundaries. The result is an utterly awesome wine!

It's almost funny that this wine is called Proprietary Red, because it sounds like the generic store version of all those fancy proprietary California reds, like Insignia, Dominus, and even Opus One. In this case, I'll grab the generic with all the impact at half the price.

Palate Primer:

V8 100% Vegetable Juice
A product of Campbell Soup Company, V8 100% Vegetable Juice is comprised of about 87% tomato juice. It includes seven other vegetables: carrots, celery, beets, parsley, lettuce, watercress, and spinach. www.v8juice.com

SIMPLY DELICIOUS

As I outlined at the start of this list, there are many differentent reasons why I selected these particular wines. Some are from regions or grapes I want to share, many take part in charitable works, and still others win out on simple deliciousness. This wine is that last one.

Many of the 2006 Riojas I'm tasting are absolute bombs—in the good sense. This wine really shows over-the-top black currant flavors on the nose, along with these beautiful Twizzlers aromas, followed by smashed strawberries. These are the big, big, big berries, the ones you find at Whole Foods that are the size of your head. Lastly, there is a little pepper coming through, which is always a nice match with strawberries. On the palate, this wine offers really amazing harmony and balance with all its elegant raspberry-strawberry flavors flowing through the mid-palate, mixed with this exotic Asian spice.

Perhaps best of all, I find this wine is not just outright delicious but also age-worthy. This wine has got CBS: complexity, backbone,

Palate Primer:

Twizzlers

Manufactured for the Hershey Company by Y&S Candies of Lancaster, Pennsylvania, Twizzlers are a "licorice-style" twisted-shape candy that comes in flavors of cherry and strawberry, as well as black licorice and chocolate.

Viñedos de Páganos, Rioja, La Nieta, 2006; $150

DOCa Rioja, Spain
Grape: Tempranillo
14.5% ABV
83 cases imported
www.eguren.com

structure. And what you need to look for in identifying a memorable, age-worthy wine is an abundance of CBS. A lot of these fruit-bomb, explosive Riojas get a bad rap, because people think their life will be shorter than Ashlee Simpson's career, but I believe that is a complete farce. This wine is not only delicious now, I see it being gorgeous over the next nine to ten years, and not reaching a beautiful plateau until it's fifteen years old.

wine country

Located in Spain's Ebro Valley, Rioja is a region of varied climates and soil, including three sub-regions Rioja Alta, Baja, and Alavesa. About 85 percent of the wines produced are red, with the Tempranillo grape accounting for more than 60 percent of the vineyards. www.riojawine.com

Honestly, nothing would make me happier than in ten years' time, long after I've forgotten about this book, to open an e-mail from somebody telling me they bought this wine and just popped it and it was superb. Mark your calendar or set an alarm in your iPhone. I am daring you to call me out on my prediction, because this wine may win on pure gorgeousness now, but I'm going to go against the crowd and say the best is yet to come.

KILLER RHÔNE ON A BUDGET

Many Wine Library TV viewers already know how I feel about the Rhône Valley region: It's absolutely one of the great value regions of the world, bursting with bright, fresh, classic wines made from blends of Grenache and Syrah. And here we have a great effort from a really excellent, progressive producer.

Côtes du Rhône-Villages is one notch above the more generic Côtes du Rhône. It's sort of like tacking those little letters onto your car to let people know it's not just a boring Honda Civic, but a Honda Civic Si model. Currently sixteen villages have been approved to use the Villages name, and Chusclan is one of them. Actually, Chusclan was one of the first, recognized back in 1953 along with names you might recognize, like Gigondas.

When I smell this wine, I immediately think of my preferred pastry: Raspberry Pop-Tarts. My grandma used to take me to all these authentic, old-school bakeries out in Queens, where they made really lofty, extravagant cakes and pastries, and I can smell that in here, too. Personally, I'm still more of a Pop-Tart guy. Then there is this ground pepper, like someone ground it all over your raspberry pastry, which sounds odd, but it's a contradiction that I really, really like.

The first thing I notice in tasting this wine is that it makes me pucker up with its great, dry tannins. It's obviously serious stuff and I think that this wine will last for three to even ten years with these

Éric Texier, Côtes du Rhône-Villages, Chusclan, 2005; $19
AOC Côtes du Rhône-Villages, France
Grapes: Grenache (50%), Syrah (50%)
13% ABV
800 cases produced
www.eric-texier.com

tannins. However, it also has the potential to be a great crowd-pleaser now because there is so much fresh, lively fruit, explosive richness, great mouthfeel, and exceptional polish. This is a wine that a lot of people will get into because it's up-front friendly, and those tannins are there but acting a little incognito. They're chilling back there in their dark sunglasses, having brunch, not being too offensive.

This wine has that combination of New World fruit and Old World backbone that I totally love. It makes me crave roast hen or a piece of venison. The best news is that if you can resist opening a few bottles for the next decade, I think you will be seriously rewarded for it. Looking into my crystal ball, with inflation and the growing demand for this sort of wine, I predict a wine like this will cost you about $40 down the line, making this killer Côtes du Rhône look like a gift.

Palate Primer:

Pop-Tarts

A product of the Kellogg Company, Pop-Tarts Toaster Pastries are rectangular pastries with a sweet filling that can be eaten immediately or warmed in the toaster. The foil package that keeps Pop-Tarts fresh was pioneered by Post with their Country Squares in 1963, using technology they developed for moist dog food. Pop-Tarts flavors include blueberry, frosted strawberry, brown sugar cinnamon, and hot fudge sundae.

THE BEST KIND OF BIRTH ANNOUNCEMENT

The importer of this wine, Aurelio Cabestrero, created a series of memorable and classic wines to mark the arrival of his son Daniel several years ago. And it looks like the celebration for his daughter is going to be equally exciting. This wine is one in a series of Spanish wines that take Christina's name. It's a tribute that any of us would be lucky to take part in, an impressive and hedonistic wine, sourced from a 150-year-old vineyard.

On the nose, there is a rainbow of flavor. We're talking Skittles along with a smorgasbord of jam. If you've ever watched jam being made, you know you first cook the jams, making them very hot before jarring them. I was fortunate enough to experience those smells when I was little with Grandma Esther, and I can smell that warm fruit in here. Actually, this smells like Grandma is getting a little crazy today and is making not just cherry and grape and raspberry but maybe even a little rhubarb jam, too. Basically, it is a hedonistic explosion of fruit on the nose, so if you like fruit, you're in for a treat.

Science Experiment:	Six-pack
If you want to really learn about cellaring wine and about your palate, buy six bottles of an age-worthy wine and taste one every two years. Log your tasting notes, and you may be stunned at how not just the wine, but also your own palate, change over time.	

Cyclo Christina, 2005; $45

DO Ribera del Duero, Spain
Grape: Tinto Fino
14% ABV
100 cases imported
www.torremilanos.com

The fruit itself is so ripe and refined, it's almost like someone cut out just the delicious centers of all your favorite fruits and is hand-feeding them to you.

The flavor is full of some serious, serious shredded dark chocolate—really impressive. It's the good stuff—80 percent cacao. This wine is also completely drying on the palate, which I really enjoy. It would be ideal with a nice rib eye or skirt steak.

Right now, this wine is leaning toward the New World, but I think some of the fruit will subside, some of the baby fat will shed, and you'll see the Old World potential start to emerge. It's just very young, which is why I'm advising Christina to not even think about touching this stuff until she is at least eight or ten years old. But even with all that bawdy fruit, this is like a punk rocker who also knows classical music. There is a serious side here that may take some time to get to know. I've tasted wines like this and seen them evolve over ten years, and I think that's the sort of fun we'll have watching Cyclo Christina grow up.

A WARHEAD OF FRUIT

If you are a dedicated fan of Old World wine, I want you to close this book, take a break, and go watch some *American Idol* with your family. This wine is not for you. But, if you enjoy the thunder, the over-the-top ripeness, and drool over cult wines from California or Australia, get ready to go totally ga ga!

This is an absolute monster of a wine. It smells like good old-fashioned Americana and cherry pie, very extracted and packed full of sugary candy. It makes me think of the five-and-dime, and that means lots and lots of candy. It smells like someone mixed blackberry and raspberry and strawberry jams together and poured them into the glass. This is truly a Skittles wine. Hello, rainbow of flavors!

The flavor of this wine is more of the same—obnoxiously fruity and hedonistically jammy. It is like Willy Wonka went on a bender and set out to make wine-flavored candy. It has such power, such ripe, indulgent flavor and syrupy texture that I could pour this over

Science Experiment:	Decanter Banter
After a few decades of aging, red wines tend to form sediment in the bottom of the bottle. Decanting is nothing more than carefully pouring the wine off the sediment into another container. However, young reds can also benefit from decanting since the addition of oxygen has the ability to open up young, powerful reds.	

Kilikanoon, Covenant Shiraz, 2005; $45
Clare Valley, South Australia
Grapes: Shiraz
15% ABV
1,500 cases imported
www.kilikanoon.com.au

my pancakes. While there is no competing with the fruit, I also don't want to imply that this wine is one-dimensional. The nice balance of tannins keeps this wine from being a pure-play of fruit. It's fake, but not overly fake. It's sort of like a really good boob job, where you don't have the scary face-lift and bleached hair and the January tan. It's just tasteful enough that it's really working for me.

Still, this is a simply massive wine that is loaded with flavor. It will last for five to ten years in the cellar with ease, and if you choose to drink it now, I think two hours of decanting will be necessary to really open it up. It is certainly a great wine for serious wine drinkers, but new wine drinkers will be totally seduced by the powerful fruit and residual sugar, so it's a wine that will please a lot of people—maybe even as many as it offends.

GOOD ENOUGH FOR THE GOTHS

When Alaric, king of the Visigoths, was passing through the Marches en route to sack Rome in 410, he's said to have stopped for a little happy hour and loaded the mules with this Verdicchio to go for his men. Since then, this white grape's fame only seems to have diminished.

But in Moncaro, Verdicchio may have finally found the PR agent it needs. Moncaro is clearly trying to show that Verdicchio has more gusto, more stamina, than most people realize. The current release of this wine, from the finest region for Verdicchio, is 2003, which is getting pretty old for a dry white wine. And if this wine is any indication, Moncaro may be set to take this grape on a global comeback tour.

There is a beautiful walnut component on the nose of this wine, along with a coffee-citrus combination, like an espresso with a bright yellow twist of lemon. It's very fresh, very clean, and I get these hints of butter and oak like the butter on buttered popcorn, but not as heavy as you'll find on many Chardonnays. The buttery oak is just dancing around in the

Label Lore

On Italian wine labels the word *classico* usually refers to wine from a smaller, more prestigious area within a larger DOC zone. This wine comes from the oldest area in Verdicchio dei Castelli di Jesi. Chianti Classico and Soave Classico have similar meanings.

Moncaro, Vigna Novali, Verdicchio dei Castelli di Jesi Classico Superiore, 2003; $24
DOC Verdicchio dei Castelli di Jesi Classico, Marche, Italy
Grapes: Verdicchio
13.5% ABV
2,500 cases produced
www.moncaro.com

aroma. I also get this ripe, papaya-mango, tropical fruit component.

On the palate—and this is where it gets exciting—this wine has dynamite acidity. The front end is loaded with pineapple. Then, in the mid-palate, there are blue stones just dancing, bouncing around my mouth like a rock tumbler. This is just a clean, crisp, fresh experience.

The Visigoths drank Verdicchio because they were going into battle, and it's what they could pillage. But imagine if those guys could walk into a wine store today, throw down a few gold coins, and buy a bottle. Think these adventurers would drink the same boring Pinot Grigio every night? No way! This wine has more complexity and flavor than 90 percent of the Pinot Grigio you're drinking. So get a little daring already. There are so many great wine options out there, so many great wines that are being ignored. This is an awesome, exciting white with a lot of new flavors to experience. Conjure your inner Visigoth. Seek and enjoy!

WINE FOR YOUR TWO-YEAR-OLD

One of the things I'm asked all the time is which wine to buy to commemorate a birth. It's a tough call. You want to invest in something that will be peaking in twenty-five years or so, when you're hopefully celebrating a wedding or graduation from medical school. That means you need serious wine. Yet you also want something that is tasty, with broad appeal, and affordable enough to grab a few bottles, maybe even a case.

Well, if you had a baby in 2005—or even if you didn't—I think this wine belongs in your cellar. The 2005 vintage was not widely declared in Portugal. In years like this, Taylor Fladgate turns to its best and most reliable vineyard, Quinta de Vargellas, and produces what is essentially a single-vineyard vintage Port. The production method and the style are identical to their vintage Port, but this wine is about half the price of a declared vintage Taylor. It does tend to be a bit lighter and slightly less long-lived, but there is no denying the quality of this vineyard to consistently produce exceptional Port. Quinta de Vargellas has been produced as a single-vineyard wine since the 1820s.

With its high intensity and huge tannins, this wine totally shocked my palate. It is beautifully rounded, with big impact on the palate, like a licorice-plum bomb exploding in my mouth. This wine is just a baby itself, but it is actually approachable now, provided you give it two to three hours of decanting before drinking. I feel that in ten

Taylor Fladgate, Quinta de Vargellas, 2005; $57
Oporto, Portugal
Grapes: Touriga Nacional, Touriga Francesa, Tinto Cão, Tinto
    Barocca
20.5% ABV
800 cases imported
www.taylor.pt

years this Port will be drinking beautifully. It will make it to the quarter-century mark without any problem. So, put this one in your cellar, forget it, and go about changing diapers, saving for college, or whatever it is you need to do. This is one small investment that is going to pay off big.

Label Lore

In general wine terms, "vintage" simply refers to the year in which the grapes were harvested. With Port, "vintage" wine is produced only when a specific Port house feels the wine has the necessary quality to age well in-bottle and the wine passes review by the Port Wine Institute. Some houses declare vintages more frequently than others, and on average a vintage is widely declared about three times per decade. The years 2000 and 2003 are the most recent widely declared vintages. Vintage Ports are among the longest-lived wines and last for decades in-bottle.
www.thevintageportsite.com

WARMING UP TO RIESLING

If you were starting a winery in California and asked me which grapes to plant, Riesling would not be in my top ten—maybe not even my top 100. Riesling belongs in California like Germans belong on surfboards. Yet, this producer has been getting the best from this grape since 1984, making some very good, varietally representative Riesling, at a price that I simply can't resist. Show me a wine that hits my sweet spot for everyday value while expressing the true character of the grape and I'm a buyer.

This Riesling has a wild mechanic and petrol nose. It's like pelting peaches in the body shop—very peachy, very copperesque, with fruit colliding with Firestone tires and oil. Unlike in Pennsylvania, we're a little too civilized to pump our own gas here in New Jersey, but this really has some of that just-topped-off-my-tank character. There is also a spoonful of beautiful green beans and English peas on the tail end of the nose.

The palate shows little hints of residual sugar, but overall the wine is quite dry, and the massive acidity just blasts that sweetness away.

Palate Primer:

Petrol

A common term for "gasoline" in the United Kingdom, petrol in regard to wine refers to an oily, kerosene, or petroleum distillate aroma. The flavor is most common in aged Riesling and is generally considered desirable.

Gainey Vineyard, Riesling Santa Ynez Valley, 2006; $14
Santa Ynez, California
Grapes: Riesling
12.8% ABV
2,600 cases produced
www.gaineyvineyard.com

Meet the Grape:
Riesling

The prized white grape of Germany, Riesling has been grown in its cool-climate homeland since at least the 1400s and is vinified in both dry and sweet styles. The grape maintains its high acid even in warmer climates, which allows it to balance rather high levels of sugar. In addition to Germany, Riesling performs well in cooler New World regions, including Alsace, Australia's Clare Valley and Monterey County, California.

This is really well made, and, best of all, it's a wine that a lot of people should be able to locate and enjoy. With this wine, I am thinking pumpkin pie, or maybe crème brûlée or apple pie or pecan pie. This is not a dessert wine in the sense that it is sweet, but in the sense that it would go well with desserts, especially fruity or autumnal desserts—almost anything that is not chocolate. California may not be my first choice for Riesling, but this wine proves that it can be done—and done well. With its low alcohol and refreshing quality, we can all be glad that this Riesling has found a home in sunny California, because when you're kickin' it Cali style this summer, this is the chilled white you want to be drinking.

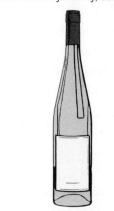

BEYOND THE FRUIT BOMBS

As people get their fill of fruit, they move on to other styles of wine. More often than not, that means Bordeaux. This gravitation toward more complex flavors is especially good for the Graves, one of the oldest and most distinctive regions, of Bordeaux.

This wine comes from an area in the northern portion of the Graves called Pessac-Léognan, delineated in 1987. Most of the prestigious wines of Graves are located here, including La Mission Haut-Brion and the Graves' first-growth Haut-Brion, which is now selling in the $400 range. Therefore, anyone seeking a taste of this region would be advised to start with this wine. For just $36, it is representative of Graves and the best effort I have ever tasted from Haut-Bergey.

I almost feel like there is a volcano of flavors in my mouth, because there is molten fruit along with extreme earthiness. This wine shows beautiful structure with blackberry and fig flavors, and it really reminds me of why I love the Graves, with the distinctive finish of snail shell and mushroomy escargot. I also love the purity of the mouthfeel and the sheer elegance that this wine brings to the table.

This wine is expertly made, and while it's not exactly cheap, it does provide great QPR. Considering the situation with the Euro/dollar and the price of its more prestigious neighbors, I don't know how much longer we'll see steals like this from Bordeaux. This wine

Château Haut-Bergey, 2005; $36
AOC Pessac-Léognan, Bordeaux, France
Grapes: Cabernet Sauvignon (65%), Merlot (35%)
13% ABV
5,800 cases produced
www.vignoblesgarcin.com
www.bobbofman.com

is very profound! So, if you've been a wine lover for a few years, and you're weary of drowning in a deluge of fruit tidal waves, this wine is going to totally hit the spot for you. Even if you're not ready to make that leap into the earthy, tobacco flavors of Graves at this point in your wine drinking, you may want to pick up this wine regardless. This Bordeaux from a legendary vintage will last for ten to fifteen years in the cellar easily. So, when you're finally ready to move beyond the fruit, Haut-Bergey will be waiting.

Meet the Grape:
Cabernet Sauvignon

Considered the noblest of red grapes, Cabernet Sauvignon has traveled widely from its homeland in Bordeaux and adapted to wine regions around the globe, most notably in California. It's capable of making red wines with great structure and tannins, resulting in long-lived wines. Cabernet Sauvignon is traditionally softened by blending with Merlot in Bordeaux.

WINE BY DEMOCRACY

Most winemaking is a dictatorship. Decisions are made by the guy with the money, or someone appointed by the guy with the money. That's what makes the approach at Foris so refreshing. In keeping with the laid-back, Northwestern disposition, winemaking is more of a family affair, including input from a "coterie" of individuals who follow the fruit from vineyard to harvest to crush to wine.

The Rogue Valley appellation is slightly off the radar of most wine lovers, overshadowed by Oregon's larger Willamette Valley. But Oregon, as a whole, is without a doubt one of the most respected Pinot Noir climates in the world. Just look at how many Burgundians have set up shop here in the last few decades. At 45 bones, this Pinot is a little pricey, but boy does it bring the Old World Burgundian love.

The nose on this wine takes some effort. It's very, very tight and not all that aromatically exciting. Dig around a bit, however, and you can find some hints of gorgeous black fruit with an underlying rugged earthiness. Look carefully, and you'll also find some rose petals and strawberries someone forgot under the bed.

The flavor of this wine is supercompact. I get the sense of a sandwich of strawberries and blackberries with a little ground pepper, smushed between old-fashioned rye bread. It just shows amazing polish and is really fresh and enchanting on the palate. There is also a very creamy coffee sensation to this wine, with a finish that is so

Foris, Rogue Valley Maple Ranch Pinot Noir, 2005; $45

Rogue Valley, Oregon
Grape: Pinot Noir
13.4% ABV
398 cases produced
www.foriswine.com

long and so elegant. The depth that this wine offers is a real throwback to the Old World Burgundian style, but the freshness, vibrancy, and purity of Oregon's fruit makes it indisputably New World.

This is the sort of wine that I would love to stick in a paper bag and present to some snobby Old World Burgundy drinkers, because no one who appreciates Pinot Noir can possibly deny that this wine totally rocks! It is just great stuff, and I think that this has another three to seven years of drinking time. I am not certain exactly who to credit for this great effort, but the team at Foris has my vote for sure.

wine country

Oregon's Rogue Valley AVA lies in a valley just 70 miles wide by 60 miles long and includes only about 20 wineries. Located in the south of Oregon along the California border, the valley is home to a great diversity of grapes, including Pinot Noir, Pinot Gris, Riesling, Gewürztraminer, Syrah, Merlot, and Cabernet Sauvignon.

RED WITH FISH

When it comes to Monopoly and driving and pairing food and wine, sometimes there are just too many rules. For instance, that whole "white with fish" thing. I find the right red wine with grilled fish can be really amazing. However, in this era of huge, overdone red wines, that "right red" can be elusive. That is where this wine strays from so many other red wines and so many other Châteauneuf-du-Papes, with its versatility, intrigue, and sheer elegance of fruit.

In this case, elegance certainly does not equal wimpy or boring. The Domaine du Banneret is a small, family-owned vineyard dating to 1405, so they have completely captured a sense of history and place in this wine, along with the "thirteen grapes symphony" that is the hallmark of Châteauneuf-du-Pape.

On the nose, there is a rusty nail component, like wrought iron or a copper penny, which is mixed in with meat blood. I get the sensation of a warm, rare steak, and you cut in and those red juices just

Domaine du Banneret, Châteauneuf-du-Pape, 2005; $50

AOC Châteauneuf-du-Pape, Rhône Valley, France

Grapes: Grenache (60%), Syrah (10%), Mourvèdre (10%), Cinsault, Muscardin, Cournoise, Clairette Rose, Bourboulenc, Picpoul, Roussanne, Terrat Noir, Picardin, Vaccarese (10% combined)

14.5% ABV

800 cases imported

domaine.banneret.free.fr

come pouring out. The blood is even a little bit gamy, like someone took my meat loaf and stuffed it with nails.

In the flavor, this wine really shows its dynamite elegance, with a beautiful, lush mouthfeel, and gorgeous raspberry and cherry flavors, with a little hint of mint on the mid-palate that is really seductive. There are these really amazing orange peel flavors that bounce around on the finish, which is dark and long, with some firm tannins. The structure is here for this wine to last easily ten to fifteen years. I would suggest decanting this wine for two or more hours before drinking it, because there is so much complexity here for it to reveal. It's delicious by itself, or could certainly handle steak, game, even lamb. Yet, the fruit is so pure and so elegant that this wine will really allow a flavorful grilled fish to shine. This is truly delicious stuff, and might just be one of the greatest steals on my list.

DÉJÀ VU ALL OVER AGAIN

Hello, 1991! I feel like I just took my *Back to the Future* DeLorean to the golden era of Hess Collection, when this wine actually meant something in the wine world and really brought the thunder. If you're not familiar, this wine was so important and so popular from 1987 to 1994 because it was selling at prices well under $20 and brought serious flavor for the money. For many drinkers, this wine came to define California Cabernet.

And with this vintage of Hess Collection, I think good times are here again, because this really is one of the finest 2005 Napa Cabernets I've tasted. The dark fruit flavors of this wine are impressive, with silky cassis; ripe, explosive grapes; and blueberries up front. On the mid-palate there is this Starbucks mocha lattè flavor with the coffee beans just bouncing around in my mouth. It serves up explosive, pure fruit without seeming artificial or fake, which is not always easy to do. There is also a pomegranate component that lingers on the finish, where the wine is at once beautifully fresh and tannic. This is one polished Cabernet!

It's also serious stuff that demands some respect. There are no happy raspberries and strawberries like you find in the flavor of so many red wines. This is all black fruit, something almost demonesque. This is not the kitschy 1960s Adam West television Batman; this is the vengeful, little-bit-scary Dark Knight Batman.

The polish and silkiness on this wine are actually very sneaky, and

Hess Collection, Cabernet Sauvignon, 2005; $50

Mount Veeder, Napa Valley, California
Grapes: Cabernet Sauvignon (94%), Merlot (4%), Malbec (2%)
14.5% ABV
9,000 cases produced
www.hesscollection.com

wine country

that's what will seduce most wine drinkers. It does have bitter, firm tannins, but laid over them is a set of violet silk sheets with your initials monogrammed on them. You just want to crawl in and snuggle up. It is really difficult to find great Napa Cabernet with this level of balance and complexity, especially at such a reasonable price. So be careful when you flirt with old lovers, because this wine is going to get you like it got me.

Mount Veeder is a subappellation of about 25 square miles located in the Mayacamas Mountains within Napa Valley. There are about 18 wineries and 1,000 acres of vineyards in Mount Veeder, with some planted on slopes as steep as 30 degrees.

Palate Primer:

Pomegranate

The fruit of a deciduous shrub, the pomegranate is cultivated throughout the Mediterranean and is also a cash crop in California. The crimson-colored fruit is berrylike in flavor, filled with seeds, and typically has a balance of sweet-tart, though is less tart than a cranberry.

THE POWER OF PINK

P art of me hates that rosé is suddenly so trendy. The problem is that a lot of rosés are pretty basic, simple and not all that exciting. No wonder pink wine gets a bad rap. But boy, did this wine just Blitzkrieg my palate. I actually love to be completely shocked.

This reminds me of an awesome candy that I adored as a kid—Now and Later, especially the watermelon flavor. That is exactly what this wine tastes like with its big juicy watermelon. I also love that this wine includes Pinotage grapes in the blend, which is somewhat unusual for a rosé. Overall, it brings serious weight with all its seductive candied watermelon flavor. But rather than being all sweet treats, mixed in with that polished candy flavor are green leaves, bringing balance and trueness to the wine. It's reminiscent of Languedoc and Provençal rosé, but with way more thunder. This

---

Palate Primer:

Now and Later

Introduced by the Phoenix Candy Company in 1962, Now and Later is a taffy-like candy that uses the slogan "Hard 'N Fruity Now and Soft 'N Chewy Later." The candy, which is popularly sold in four-piece squares, is now manufactured by Farley's and Sathers Candy Company, and in addition to watermelon has flavors of apple, cherry, peach smash, banana, black radberry, and more.
    www.farleysandsathers.com

Slowine, Rosé, 2007; $13
Overberg, South Africa
Grapes: Pinot Noir (49%), Pinotage (39%), Shiraz (12%)
12.5% ABV
1,000 cases imported
www.slowine.co.za

wine is a vacation in the South of France, but you're kicking it with Barry Bonds!

This wine also begs for sushi. As I am drinking this right now, I'm totally dying for sea urchin. Another bit of advice: Don't be afraid to try this wine a little warmer than usual. I'm actually enjoying it near room temperature. This is not your first high-school beer, where you really don't like the taste, so you make it icy cold and gulp it down; believe me, you *want* to taste this. Drink it too cold and you'll miss out on the great flavors of small strawberries, yellow raspberries, those green leaves turning yellow in fall, even a bit of acorn. I may love Now and Later, but this wine has plenty of flavor and intensity that make it more than just candy.

Label Lore

Slowine is a joint project by a group of like-minded wine-makers and neighbors around the Groenland Mountain, South Africa. The image on their labels is of a local parrot-beaked tortoise, which goes more often by the affectionate Afrikaans term *padlopertjie*, or "small road-walker."

BREAKIN' THE LAW

There are certain rewards to following the law and being a good boy. For instance, you get to list all sorts of nice stuff on your résumé. In the case of wine, that includes things like a prestigious wine region and a vintage year. But this wine went on spring break to Costa and never came back. It said screw off to The Man.

Because the winemakers combine secondary fruit from three different vintages to make the best possible wine, they can't put a year on the bottle. Instead it has essentially a batch number, "XV." You'll occasionally see nonvintage $7 wines, like Marietta Old Vines, but when it comes to marketing $40 wines, a move like this could mean death. By using grapes across vintages, they also forfeit any chance of listing the Barbaresco region and are reduced to a label that reads Vino di Tavola, or "table wine."

But these are exactly the types of changes and chances I want to be part of, especially when they succeed like this. This wine is people having the confidence and sheer guts to do what they believe in. Just as an Italian opera combines elements of solo singing, chorus, drama,

VAYNERCABULARY

A^2—(adjective) Aromatically Awesome. A wine's aroma is an integral part of the tasting experience. A wine that is A^2 invites you to drink it and portends great flavors to come.

Roagna, Opera Prima XV; $48
VdT, Italy
Grape: Nebbiolo di Barbaresco
13% ABV
500 cases produced
www.roagna.com

and dancing, this wine is a performance, bringing together the best talents across several vintages.

One thing I love about this wine is the charcoal on the nose. The XIII had it, the XIV had it, and the XV has it. (And you thought you only needed Roman numerals to read movie copyrights.) I smell almost a chalky cellar-dust smoky quality. It's like we're barbecuing berries. The nose also has a very interesting, pretty floral character. There are lilac and rose petals, but it's so intense that it almost reminds me of that Dollar Store potpourri I bought for Mother's Day when I was seven years old. In a word, this wine is A^2.

On the palate, the XV is tremendously balanced, with extraordinarily firm tannins. They are almost firm to a fault. I say "almost," because just when you think this wine is going to a place where it will be undrinkable, in comes a waterfall of blueberry custard, like something out of Willy Wonka's factory. I want to eat this wine. I want to bite into the glass and eat it. They were daring enough to make it. Shouldn't you be daring enough to taste it?

EXPENSIVE, BUT WORTH IT

From my first sip of this wine, it just killed me with pleasure, and it only gets better from there. The way I describe the aroma of this wine is lollipop clouds; it has an almost angelic nose: fluffy and ethereal, like cotton candy. It is just so pretty, with a combination of Tootsie Rolls and cherry on the nose. It's actually like a Tootsie Roll Pop. Remember those? Where the kid would go ask that owl how many licks it takes to get to the center of a Tootsie Pop? Man, that thing really freaked me out.

Above all, this wine shows balance. And at the end of the day, the greatest things on this earth are about balance and harmony—in wine, in food, in life. This wine is a tightrope walker, with all its balance, polish, refinement, and poise. It is one of the most impressive wines on this list for that reason alone.

Palate Primer:

Tootsie Roll Pop

A chocolaty, chewy candy, the Tootsie Roll was introduced in New York City by Leo Hirshfield in 1896. Incredibly, the Tootsie Roll has remained unchanged in flavor and price for 109 years—they still cost only 1 cent. Tootsie Roll Industries introduced the Tootsie Roll Pop in 1931 and today are the world's largest manufacturer of lollipops. The iconic owl commercial first appeared in 1970. www.tootsie.com

Finca Allende, Rioja Aurus, 2005; $215
DOCa Rioja, Spain
Grapes: Tempranillo (85%), Graciano (15%)
14% ABV
50 cases imported
www.finca-allende.com

There is one problem. This wine is expensive. It may be out of reach for many people, but if ever there was a reason to miss a car payment, this is it. This wine really strikes a harmonious chord with me, making it deserving of great food. When I think about my favorite restaurants—The French Laundry, Charlie Trotter's, Gotham Bar and Grill—this is the wine I want to enjoy with their cuisine. I think this wine has the balance and flexibility to adjust to almost any dish. If this wine were a superhero, it would be Plastic Man.

On the finish, there is an amazing blackberry jam component, and that fruit is just as clear now as the second the wine hit my palate. When you get into wines like this, showing flavors that last through two- to three-minute finishes, you are getting into magical stuff. Yes, this wine is expensive, but perhaps not when you consider I would put this up against some of the great young first-growth Bordeaux—Lafite and Latour—I've been drinking. In the wine world, compliments don't get much better than that.

A DAY WINEMAKING AT THE BEACH

#29

wine country

Fiefs Vendéens is one of only a handful of French wine regions designated as a VDQS, an acronym for Vin Délimité de Qualité Supérieure (Delimited Wine of Superior Quality). VDQS was created in 1949 as an intermediary status between Vin de Pays (VdP) and Appellation d'Origine Controlée (AOC) wine. Most VDQS wines have moved on to AOC status, so the designation is actually the most rare one in France today, representing somewhere around 1 percent of French wine.

This is another off-the-beaten-path Pinot. In fact, rather than a path, you'd be better off with a boat. These vineyards are on land that was formerly a part of the extensive salt marsh network surrounding Ile d'Olonne (Olonne Island). The soil is so sandy that these vines must be trained low to the ground and almost appear to be growing on the beach—no surprise, since this area is a major tourist destination. The cooling breezes of the Atlantic and unique microclimate allow Pinot Noir to thrive in this unlikely place, even if you do have to get on your hands and knees to pick it. So, it's always great to see Pinot Noir, a grape that is known for being fickle, thriving and producing distinctive wine outside of Burgundy.

There is some really bright fruit on the front end of this wine, along with a pretty green broccoli component, fresh sawdust, and cellar floor–type flavors. And, of course, there is classic ripe cherry fruit. This wine is simply a beautiful example of what Pinot Noir can

Domaine St-Nicolas Fiefs Vendéens, "Cuvée Jacques," 2005; $25

VDQS Fiefs Vendéens, Loire Valley, France

Grapes: Pinot Noir

12.5% ABV

500 cases imported

www.domaine-saint-nicolas.com

be when people aren't cheating and mixing other grapes with it. It's very clean, very fresh, with explosive cassis and tobacco flavors dancing together on the mid-palate. There is just this really great integration of bark, tobacco, and Asian spices on the finish. This Pinot is very lush and explosive without being overly ripe.

That kind of balance means it would be a great complement for food, even some hearty fish. I would love to be enjoying this with cod or trout. Or perhaps some Atlantic fish. After all, this wine is practically a product of the sea.

VAYNERCABULARY

Wine bully (n)—*One who uses their knowledge of wine to abuse others. Knowing what VDQS means in the French wine system is cool; correcting your grandma on it makes you a wine bully.*

#28 BORDEAUX EMBRACES PORTUGAL

Nothing validates your upcoming wine country status like having the Bordelaise move in. For wine lovers, the partnership between Bruno Prats, Bordeaux winemaker and former owner of Château Cos d'Estournel (see page 200) and the Port maestro Charles Symington, whose family has Graham's, Warre's, and Dow's, to name a few, is more exciting than Charles marrying Diana in 1981. (Sorry, one of you guys has to wear the tiara.)

The 2005 vintage of Chryseia flaunts its pedigree and is, without a doubt, one of the most interesting wines I've tasted this year. There are other good wines from Portugal out there, even in this book, but this particular wine convinces me that the Portuguese are serious about competing on a very high level and are here to stay. This wine features the same grapes found in great Port, and they perform amazingly, even without any fortification. The raspberry aromas are explosive and dominant.

On the palate, the hedonistic fruit transitions into a greenness—bell pepper, asparagus, and English peas. This wine really walks that tightrope of balance between Old World and New World, so I think it will find fans across the board. The viscosity and

Label Lore

The word *douro* literally means "golden" or "of gold." When the partnership set out to make an iconic Greek wine, they chose the Greek word *chryseia*, which has the same meaning.

Prats & Symington, Chryseia Douro, 2005; $73
DO Douro, Portugal
Grapes: Touriga Nacional (70%), Touriga Franca,
    Tinta Roriz (30%)
13% ABV
2,541 cases produced
www.chryseia.com

mouthfeel are amazing: extremely rich and palate-coating. I feel as if I am more chewing it than drinking it. And the finish is plush and velvety, with the structure to last for fifteen years.

This wine also gives a nod to Bordeaux in its marketing. Not only is it expensive, but with a relatively small production, the wine is offered in future sales, much like the greats of Bordeaux. It is, in fact, only the second non-Bordeaux, non-French wine to be sold by the leading Bordeaux négociants. This is neither Port nor Bordeaux, but combines great attributes of both of these powerful wines in one of those unexpected marriages that seems so right.

Meet the Grape:
Touriga Franca

Often referred to as Touriga Francesa, this grape is lighter and more aromatic than the more structured Touriga Nacional. It is also the most widely planted grape in Douro, produces consistent yields, and is valued for adding floral aromas to the blend in both Port and table wine.

COOL IT WITH THE ICE BUCKET!

I feel as if I need to take this opportunity to make a little public service announcement: *Hey, kids! Gary Vay-ner-chuk here! Like most of America, you're probably overchilling your white wines. If you drink your white wines too cold, you're missing out on flavor and wasting money. Gary says: If you overchill, you might as well drink swill. And that's one to grow on!*

As I sit tasting in my office, this wine is at room temperature, and it is still tasting good enough to secure a place in my top 101 wines. The aroma offers a gorgeous explosion of honey and graham cracker, like I'm in a 1980s cereal commercial. There is also a grainy, flowery, weedy smell coming through, along with a little hint of caramel and butterscotch.

On the palate, the lemon and honey elements take total control. I really love the flavor combination this wine puts together. If there are any *Top Chef* competitors reading, I want to offer you a great dessert inspiration: You absolutely need to combine honeydew melon, lemon, and honey with a graham cracker crust. Actually, I can't guarantee it

Label Lore

Founded by Richard Sanford and Thekla Brumder, Alma Rosa Winery & Vineyards includes an organic vineyard situated on an original Mexican land grant named Rancho Santa Rosa. In Spanish *alma* means "soul," therefore the name refers to their view that these wines are the soul of the ranch.

Alma Rosa, Pinot Blanc La Encantada Vineyard, 2005; $30
Santa Rita Hills, California
Grape: Pinot Blanc
14.1% ABV
352 cases produced
www.almarosawinery.com

Meet the Grape:
Pinot Blanc

As a mutation of Pinot Gris—and therefore Pinot Noir—Pinot Blanc produces full-bodied white wines that are high in acid and restrained in aroma. The grape has been largely phased out in its homeland of Burgundy, but is abundant in Italy, where it goes by Pinot Bianco, as well as in Argentina, Uruguay, and California, where it is largely confined to Monterey County.

will make a winning dessert, but it makes one fantastic wine. The honey-butterscotch-caramel component in this wine is almost reminiscent of an ice cream topping. Yet, the flavors remain very fresh and floral on the finish, with hints of sunflower seeds. This grape variety is under the radar, and that is a shame, because it is showing great complexity and backbone.

If you pay attention to the white wines on this list—the wines that excite me above all others—you'll see a pretty consistent theme. Most of them have great weight, a super mouthfeel, lovely acidity, and sheer exuberance. Now, if you want to stick them in the refrigerator overnight, put them into deep freeze, and miss out on all of that, be my guest. But I'm suggesting you warm up to these whites.

A SUPERIOR BORDEAUX

Unlike many of the other Bordeaux on my list, this wine does not come from a prestigious Commune or appear in *Who's Who of Bordeaux Snobs*, also known as the 1855 Classification. It was this list that crowned wines like Lafite and Latour as well as Château Cos d'Estournel as Bordeaux's best. However, outside of these few estates, there is a ton of generic Bordeaux and Bordeaux Supérieur out there—so much that it accounts for about 25 percent of the AOC wine in France. This wine proves that these are not second-class citizens.

Yves Vatelot released his first Château Reignac in 1996, and in 2002 he purchased a small property of 35-year-old Merlot vines, which now produces Balthus. When I visited Yves in May 2007, he blew me away with his thought process, vision, and desire for quality. He uses a patented system of rotating barrels containing juice and grape pomace (skins and the other crap that is not juice) during fermentation, which gives this wine superb structure and expressive

Palate Primer:

Phillies Cigars

Created in Philadelphia over a century ago, Phillies are popular value-priced cigars sold at convenience stores and gas stations. The popular blunt size comes in flavors like Blunt Banana, Blunt Berry, Blunt Chocolate Aroma, and Blunt Coconut.

Château Reignac, Cuvée Balthus, 2005; $78
AOC Bordeaux Supérieur, France
Grape: Merlot
14.5% ABV
400 cases produced
www.reignac.com
www.bobbofman.com

flavors. Some people might cringe at the thought of basic Bordeaux Supérieur nearing 80 bones, but I find this wine a value. If anything, it is *underpriced*!

Balthus, like many great Bordeaux, comes from one small plot of grapes—only about 7.5 acres. They simply can't make any more. With demand rising from Asia, Russia, and China, and the dollar looking about as worthless as wampum, Bordeaux prices are heading in only one direction.

This wine is so inky and dark it is clearly an octopus wine. On the palate, beautiful blueberries are dancing around in my mouth with a quadruple shot of espresso. You have major Starbucks flavors, along with some Green Mountain Coffee, some Burger King Joe, and maybe even a little Dunkin' Donuts for Rachael Ray. In addition to the elegant fruit, there is some cheap cigar wrapper. This is no Monte-cristo—more like the Phillies or García y Vega that your college pals would do other things with. On the tail end there is more tobacco, some soy sauce, and Asian spice, with a real sharp edge. This wine has lots of pizzazz and gives a little kick in your pants on the way out. This Supérieur is not inferior!

A CHARDONNAY SUBSTITUTE

Chardonnay is one of the great white grapes, and as such there are plenty in this book, including entries from France, Hungary, and New Zealand. However, I'm always encouraging white wine drinkers to look at grapes other than Chardonnay. The problem for many drinkers weaned on Chardonnays is that these wines are often so creamy, so lush, that when I try to turn these Chard junkies on to Pinot Grigio, or Sauvignon Blanc, or Riesling, they say something like, "Heck, Gary, why don't I just drink water?"

Well, this wine is my answer to all those heavy-on-the-palate white fans who can't get beyond Chardonnay, because this Viognier is like Chardonnay on the planet Jupiter, with its massive weight and full body, along with an explosive acidity that is lacking in many other examples.

What this wine also has is gorgeous aromatic complexity. Rideau specializes in Rhône varietal wines, which I feel is a great niche because white Rhône grapes are producing some of the most interesting wines from California at the moment. Viognier may be at the top of that short list, although this winery also dabbles in Marsanne and Roussanne.

The nose of this wine is totally fascinating, with a mix of grains meets apples. I feel like I'm enjoying freshly sliced apples on top of

Rideau Vineyard, In-Circle Cellar Club Estate Viognier, 2006; $36

Santa Ynez Valley, California
Grape: Viognier
14.6% ABV
900 cases produced
www.rideauvineyard.com

my healthy Whole Foods cereal that cost me like $9 for a little box. There is also a touch of oiliness that hints at that weight to come on the palate, almost an olive oil component. The flavor offers bold green apples, lively hints of vanilla, and a gorgeous iceberg lettuce component on the mid-palate. The finish on this wine is also extremely long, vibrant, and fruity. A minute after drinking it I am *still* being bowled over by tropical flavors of mango and pineapple. This wine measures up to many serious Rhône whites I've tasted in the $60 range.

Believe it or not, I can see a white of this magnitude lasting for three to four years, and I think this wine would be great with charred fish over the next several years. If you are a Chardonnay fan who has avoided other whites because you found them too thin or wimpy, I challenge you to try this wine. No more excuses.

Palate Primer:

Iceberg Lettuce

Also known as Crisphead, Iceberg is one of the six commonly recognized lettuce cultivars, identifiable by its tight, cabbage-like head. Iceberg is a mild lettuce with a crunchy texture and refreshing flavor and takes its name from an era when it was transported covered in crushed ice.

BOWLED OVER BY BAROLO

I fell in love with this producer for their 2001 effort, and tasting this wine now reminds me of why I admire them and totally adore Barolo. When it comes to very high quality, premium wine, the Nebbiolo-based wines of Piemonte—with Barolo as their king—might represent some of the best values in the world. These wines are simply extraordinary.

On the nose in particular, there is nothing to rival a beautiful Barolo. I feel like some kid just got home from soccer practice, took off his sweaty sock, and went to the refrigerator to fill it with cherries, raspberries, blackberries, and strawberries, like he was making a jailhouse weapon. Then he just started swinging that sock and slammed me in the mouth with the wallop of Thor's hammer. That Piemonte funkiness is in the mix, but you cannot deny the massive Skittles rainbow fruit punch. At the same time, the nose is very fresh. I almost get the sense of wintergreen and water mist, like that great feeling when you're shopping the produce aisle and suddenly those water misters kick in.

The flavor of this wine is just outrageously good! The beautiful tannins are right up in front, but knowing Barolo, I can already envision how in three to five years this stuff will drink like silk. There is beautiful black, tannic, cocoa-driven structure in the mid-palate, which gives way to red fruit on the finish. This is a delightful, delicious home run of a wine. The character, structure, backbone, and

Bartolomeo, Barolo, 2004; $60
DOCG Barolo, Italy
Grape: Nebbiolo
14% ABV
300 cases produced
www.piemonte.dk

blueprint of a classic wine are all in place here.

Despite its size, I think this wine will be very flexible with food, which is one of the hallmarks of Barolo. This wine will stand up to your biggest steak, but is still versatile enough to pair with fish, especially after mellowing for a few years. You know what I really want right now, however? Liver. Some old-school Russian liver and onions—the type of food that put everyone in the Old Country in the ground at the age of 50. Liver, onions, and Bartolomeo Barolo—now there are a few of my favorite things!

Meet the Grape: Nebbiolo

With a name derived from the Italian word *nebbia*, or "fog," Nebbiolo makes its home in the foggy foothills of Piemonte. While small plantings exist outside of Italy, Nebbiolo is best known as the grape for the DOCG wines Barolo and Barbaresco, notable for their powerful tannins, high acidity, and exceptional quality.

#23 BIG SHOES TO FILL

My father is an amazing and much-loved guy, and I try to live up to his example every day. That's why I can empathize with Kirk Venge. In addition to being Kirk's dad, Nils Venge is a Napa Valley pioneer who worked at Charles Krug, Sterling, and Villa Mount Eden before personally inaugurating Napa Valley into a place of prestige with his 1985 Groth Reserve Cabernet Sauvignon—the first California wine to earn 100 points from Robert M. Parker Jr.

Fortunately, Kirk, who is the primary winemaker at Venge Vineyards, has no shortage of talent himself and fully deserves his reputation as one of the hot, young, up-and-coming winemakers in the region. I have a huge amount of respect for both these guys and their stable of tasty wines. I think this blend of three dynamic grapes, however, is one of the most fun, affordable, and beautiful in its conception.

This wine is so strikingly dark in the glass that the color alone arouses me. On the nose, I smell a distinctive cream of wheat, along with licorice, liqueur, and almost a Kir Royale aroma that is very dense, dark, and black with its fruit.

On the palate, this wine is totally hedonistic. You can't help but be blown away by its uppity cherries. The flavor is like a cherry exposition. It makes me wish I were a cherry connoisseur so that I could rattle off the fifteen primary varieties of cherries—because they are all in here. There are sweet ones, sour ones; black, red, and yellow

Venge Vineyards, Scouts Honor Red, 2005; $40
Napa Valley, California
Grapes: Zinfandel (68%), Petite Sirah (15%), Charbono (17%)
15.1% ABV
310 cases produced
www.vengevineyards.com

ones. But beyond the delicious fruit, the beautiful balance, the great structure, and very, very pleasant mouthfeel are probably the most exciting aspects of this wine. On the back end there is just the right touch of a fielder's glove: a fresh, leathery flavor.

As far as California Zinfandel goes, this wine is not cheap, but it's actually one of the lower-priced wines from this rather small producer. To all those people who love Zin from Ravenswood, Ridge, and Seghesio, I really hope you'll give this a try. It offers the sort of focused fruit you already adore, but the addition of Petite Sirah and Charbono make it an exciting and different experience. This is an effort that shows more talent, dedication, and ability than a straight-A report card. It would make any father proud.

Meet the Grape:
Charbono

Also known as Bonarda in Argentina, where it is widely planted, this grape makes dark-colored and acidic wines. In California, Charbono is relatively scarce and is rarely bottled as a varietal wine.

BEAUJOLAIS, BUT NOT NOUVEAU

The Beaujolais Nouveau phenomenon, as successful as it's been in America, is really like a dark, dangerous, angry cloud over all of Beaujolais. And it's time that America gets off its ass and realizes that Beaujolais is real wine, not just some bubble-gum-flavored excuse for a party. This particular wine is from a single vineyard located in one of the ten Beaujolais crus. I first tasted this wine late in the afternoon, after a typical day sorting through hundreds of wines for this book, and it just blew my face off.

On the aroma, the rosemary and strawberry are just dancing—not exactly waltzing, more like a little hip-hop number to LL Cool J's "Rock the Bells." Beautiful floral aromas of roses and lilacs just keep coming at me, along with aromas of a fresh rhubarb pie and little hints of black pepper. It's just so clean and so gorgeous.

The flavor is full of beautiful, complex fruit, with a slight soapy quality. It's like Mr. Bubbles meets Smucker's jam. It is just such a nice drink, and I am desperate for people to realize how good the Gamay grape, and also Louis Jadot, can be. Because of their

Palate Primer:

Mr. Bubbles

A product of TootsieToy, Mr. Bubbles will be 75 years old in 2008. The soapy solution is a favorite of children, and is also used in professional arrangements by Cirque du Soleil. www.mrbubbles.com

Maison Louis Jadot, Château des Jacques, Clos de Rochegrès, 2006; $32

AOC, Moulin-à-Vent, Beaujolais, France

Grape: Gamay

13.5% ABV

250 cases imported

www.louisjadot.com

Beaujolais-Villages and Pouilly-Fuissé and the other standard stuff they make, Jadot is a tricky winery. They get pissed on by a lot of people, and sometimes rightfully so. But when you make wine like this, which brings so much flavor and complexity and richness in a medium-bodied red, I love you.

People need to realize that Beaujolais is part of Burgundy, and wines like this can bring real excitement and enormous quality to the table. I am incredibly excited about this wine, because it is really, really well made. And, it's absolute proof of what the Gamay grape can do. So I'm pleading with you, put down the Nouveau and go grab some serious Beaujolais.

Meet the Grape:
Gamay

The principal grape of Beaujolais, Gamay, generally makes light-bodied, fruity red wines, but it can also produce richer, longer-lived wines, most notably in the Beaujolais crus. The cultivation of Gamay was famously banned in Burgundy in favor of Pinot Noir by Duke of Burgundy Philippe the Bold in 1395.

FROM RUINS TO RICHES

I am a very young guy in the wine world. And by the time I reach 45 or 50, the age of most of today's wine establishment, I think we'll be looking at a very different global wine landscape. I have no doubt that great wines will emerge from China, India, and Brazil, and in the U.S. from Arizona, Texas, and New Mexico. Let's face it: Twenty-five years ago, absolutely nobody dreamed of the success of New Zealand Sauvignon Blanc. So this wine from Lebanon is the sort of story that opens my mind—and my eyes—to the future.

My mom actually refers to me as the Messiah, but in this case, *massaya* is the Arabic word for "twilight" in Lebanon's Bekaa Valley. The Bekaa Valley has been a producer of fine wine since ancient times, so I'm totally excited to see such amazing modern wines, like this Massaya, with the potential to return the region to prominence. That's the sworn mission of brothers Sami and Ramzi Ghosn, who have rejuvenated their family's war-torn estate with the winemaking assistance of Frédéric and Daniel Brunier, owners of Domaine du Vieux Télégraphe in Châteauneuf-du-Pape.

But all that pedigree means nothing to me if you don't have the goods, and this wine brings the thunder: great licorice, dark raspberry, and some wild berries. It tastes like these little berries that grew wild in the woods in New Jersey. They are not real big, not real perfect, maybe a little sour, but you find them and they are still delicious and intense. There is also a little oak monster, but he's

Massaya, Gold Reserve, 2004; $35

Bekaa Valley, Lebanon

Grapes: Cabernet Sauvignon (50%), Mourvèdre (40%), Syrah (10%)

13.5% ABV

1,000 cases imported

www.massaya.com

tame enough to be your friend. He's like a baby tiger, a cute house pet because you know he's too small to really turn on you. On the palate, the fruit is like blackberry jam, a little like an overcooked pie, with a nice cinnamon mid-palate. And there is a great, long finish of chocolate-covered cherries that I really enjoy. This wine is just a huge fruit bomb, which is not always my cup of tea, but it has enough balance that I am really excited about it.

If you are a big fan of California cult Cabernet, this is my gift to you. You can enjoy something awesome, from a different area, and at an even better price point. For Lebanon, the future is now.

wine country

In modern history, the Bekaa Valley is best known as the site of armed conflict and drug smuggling, but its role as a wine-producing region dates to Roman times. In the Valley lie the Roman ruins at Baalbeck, including the impressive temple of Bacchus, the Roman god of wine.

GREEK REVIVAL

I f you have not heard about the renaissance taking place in Greek winemaking, you're missing out. I've already visited Greece once and have another trip planned to delve deeper into these exciting wines. And more than any other grape, Moschofilero has the potential to do for Greece what Grüner Veltliner did for Austria—put it on the international wine map. I am totally excited about the potential of this country—and this grape—to produce truly great white wines.

This wine really impressed me with its beautiful richness, acidic balance, and overall harmony. When you think of Greece—the location and the climate—you think of shellfish, salads, and lighter fare, this wine, with its freshness and low alcohol, makes the perfect companion. On the nose, it has almost a gingerbread-man component, with really pretty ginger and spice aspects going on. There is also some seashell, imparting a sense of saltiness, which is really exciting. It's very different, very vibrant, and very fresh.

On the palate, this wine is crisp, dry, and pinpoint accurate with its lemon-lime flavors. Choose your soda—Sprite, 7UP, even Squirt. There is this really pronounced, heavy lime component that I like quite a bit. It really follows through on the finish, and if you are a fan of lime flavor, you need to seek this wine out. This wine is also very clean, which is a great compliment for a wine of this body type. Under the lime, there is a slight flavor of pear skin that I really enjoy. There

Domaine Tselepos, Moschofilero, 2006; $18
AOC Mantinia, Greece
Grapes: Moschofilero
11.5% ABV
16,000 cases produced
www.tselepos.gr

is a real difference between pear and the skin of the pear, because the skin has some extra bitterness. There is also some white asparagus flavors, which I like a whole lot. It's really all in harmony, making this wine exotic, different, clean, and refreshing.

This is total porch wine, one that you can sip and chill out with and not have to think too hard about. The world needs more porch wines, at least more that are *not* New Zealand Sauvignon Blanc. So, here's something a little different that will bring some variety to your porch swing or your summer seafood salad.

Meet the Grape: Moschofilero

An aromatic white grape, Moschofilero often draws flavor comparisons to Muscat or Traminer, although it is unrelated. The grayish grape is capable of producing wines that range from clear to silvery yellow or even pink, and it is regarded as one of the Greek grapes with the greatest potential for international success.

WHEN CHENIN TALKS, I LISTEN

With this wine you have an underrated grape (Chenin Blanc) from an underrated appellation (Savennières) in an underrated region (the Loire Valley). Even for people who know about and appreciate the Loire Valley, Savennières is not one of the first places that pops to mind—which is all the more reason you should embrace this wine. I truly love this wine, and I believe the wines of Chenin Blanc in general are some of the most interesting in the world. I think of Chenin Blanc as the really bright kid in high school who wasn't considered supercool and rarely got a word in edgewise at the table, but had something really great to add to the conversation if you'd just take a minute and listen.

On the nose, there is a clear sense of tangerine peel and crisp Red Delicious apples. There is also an almost medicinal component that I really like, like a subtle hint of Vicks VapoRub. It almost smells like heated plastic, like someone is melting your Wiffle ball. The classic apples and pears are at the forefront, but all this plastic and medicine make the wine's aroma truly intriguing.

Now for the taste: *Pow!* Aluminum bat! When I drink Chenin Blanc in this style, it always makes me think of college baseball. Something about the way this grape attacks my palate makes me think of steel and aluminum. It's actually more like I'm one of the New York gangs in the 1979 cult-classic movie *The Warriors* and one of the guys from the rival gang just hit me in the mouth with a metal pipe. But don't

Domaine du Closel—Château des Vaults, Savennières la Jalousie, 2006; $22

AOC Savennières, France
Grapes: Chenin Blanc
13.5% ABV
5,000 cases imported
www.savennieres-closel.com

take any of this as a negative. The wine is really very fresh. Let's imagine that rival gang member took my favorite baseball bat and washed it down with kiwi juice and then hit me in the mouth. So I'm like, thanks man, I kinda sort of enjoyed that. Let me have another.

There are also hints of bluestone, very fresh aquariumesque flavors, like a freshwater aquarium tank that's really alive with all the pebbles and stones and shells, with hints of the Atlantic Ocean. If you don't already know and love Chenin Blanc, this is a great place to start.

Meet the Grape:
Chenin Blanc

Perhaps the most versatile of grapes, Chenin Blanc is capable of making dry table wines, sparkling wine, and rich, demi-sec dessert wines, which it does ably in the Loire Valley. In the Loire, it often goes by the name Pineau de la Loire, and in South Africa, where it also performs well, it is often labeled as Steen.

AN ITALIAN STALLION

Although QPR (that's quality to price ratio) is very important to me in selecting wines, that does not mean all great wines are going to be affordable. Some wines are 100 bucks and worth it. This wine approaches that three-figure price tag, but it is just so good that it willed itself to victory on this list.

On the nose, you can't deny the dry-roasted peppers and cherry aromas. There is also a secondary flavor of V8 juice. It's subtle, but I really enjoy it. You give me vegetables and tomato juice any day and I'm a happy boy. There is also a beautiful, vibrant citrus component, but what I enjoy most is this overriding flavor of classic pipe tobacco smell. You don't often get to smell a pipe nowadays, and this takes me back to the late 1970s and I'm hanging out at the track with Lucky Louie, sporting his mutton chops and puffing his pipe. So more often than not, dropping $100 on a bottle of wine is a waste of money, but this one is worth every cent.

If you're still really apprehensive about the price, open the bottle

Palate Primer:

Pipe Tobacco

Much in the way a winemaker blends grapes to balance and improve a wine, a tobacconist may combine various types of tobacco, like Burley, Virginia, Latakia, and Perique, to craft complex and richly layered house blends.

La Gerla, Brunello di Montalcino Riserva, 2003; $80
DOCG Brunello di Montalcino, Italy
Grape: Sangiovese
14% ABV
200 cases imported
www.lagerla.it

and leave it on the counter for twenty-four hours before drinking it. The wine will only get better and you'll have 10 bucks' worth of air freshener to make yourself feel better.

This wine has what I call passionate plum flavors—very, very plummy. If you are of Hungarian descent, you'll know about *gwetche kuchen*, plum cakes, and you can smell those baking plums in this wine. On the palate, this wine is bone dry, with bitterly dry tannins that will carry this baby for twelve to fifteen years with ease. But perhaps most impressive is this wine's structure. It has the body of a Greek god, like one of those kids you'll see at the NFL combines— young, fit, and sculpted from top to bottom. It's got the nose, bouquet, targeted attacks, tannins, structure—just everything going for it. And it's not like this wine was a natural, because 2003 was a very hot and difficult vintage throughout Europe. I think winemaker Vittorio Fiore saw the potential here and put this wine through the paces. He had these grapes doing not just pushups, but situps and lunges, and really made this wine into a specimen. I want to grab the guy, congratulate him, and kiss him on the lips, because this wine is gonna go far.

CHIANTI LETS IT RIDE

When I first saw this wine, I was yucked out by the $45 price. That is some seriously expensive Chianti, and I had real doubts about how this wine was possibly going to deliver that kind of value. But then I thought to myself, many Super-Tuscans, like this wine, are mostly Sangiovese; they top this price all the time. Let's see what Chianti Classico can bring. Well, I am here to tell you that this wine is not your grandpappy's straw-bottomed jug of Chianti.

In order to make this wine so rich, so intense, Dievole takes some serious risks, like allowing the grapes to hang in the vineyards until they are almost beginning to raisin, creating an Amarone-like wine. It has meat and cheese aromas, green olive meets Parmigiano Reggiano on the nose. There is also a hint of leather, almost like the smell you get from your leather swivel chair at your computer.

But the extraordinary mouthfeel is where this wine really wins me

Palate Primer:

Jolt Cola

Created in 1985 by the Jolt Cola Company of Rochester, New York, Jolt Cola was originally marketed with the slogan "All the sugar and twice the caffeine." The current Jolt product line is available in 23.5-ounce cans and includes flavors of Cola, Blue Raspberry, Cherry Bomb, and Silver (lemon-lime).

Dievole, Chianti Classico Riserva Novecento, 2004; $37

DOCG Chianti Classico Riserva, Italy

Grapes: Sangiovese (90%), Tuscan grapes, including Canaiolo, Mammoto, Colorino, and Malvasia Nera (10%)

13.5% ABV

3,533 cases produced

www.dievole.it

over. It is extremely luscious, with ripe, bold, explosive tannins that completely take over your mouth. From the very first sip, this wine just sucks every drop of moisture from your mouth, so this is very much a food wine. On the flavor, it has beautiful raisin, almost prunelike flavors, hints of plum, and orangey spice. I also get a little shot of raspberry mocha, almost like a Blue Raspberry Jolt soda. But that soda element integrates really nicely with all the forest flavors—woods and sticks and leaves—and the core components of raisins, plums, and dates.

I need to emphasize that even at 37 bones, this wine offers good value because it is in a league with some of the world's top wines. That also means it will last seven to ten years in the cellar. In fact, I almost wish it came with a red warning sticker that read "Do not open before 2010." If you're rolling with the cellar—Jay-Z style—then put this one away and forget about it. If you have to open it now, you're going to need a rack of lamb to get through the bottle, but you are going to absolutely love it.

RAISIN JUICE

wine country

The Barossa is Australia's most recognized wine region and includes both the Barossa Valley, where Shiraz is king, and the Eden Valley, where cooler temperatures are more suitable for Riesling. The Barossa is home to such Aussie pioneers as Jacob's Creek, Penfold's, Wolf Blass, Henschke, and Yalumba, and includes Shiraz vines dating to the 1840s. www.barossa.com

I don't know if we can even call this wine, but we're gonna try. This is a fortified wine made by letting the Shiraz grapes hang on the vine until they are shriveled, dry, and concentrated. Then, during fermentation, distilled spirits are added to cut short the fermentation, boost the alcohol, and lock in the sweetness of the fruit. This is the same way that Port is made, but the flavor that Wayne Dutschke captures with this wine is entirely original.

On the nose, there is alcohol, wasabi, soy sauce. It legitimately smells like a sushi bar with everything but the sushi. The palate offers similar flavors, with a hedonistic syrupy component that is so exciting it's almost overwhelming. With 18 percent alcohol, all this sugar syrup and chewy fruit is just a total bomb. The dried raisin character of the grapes is captured beautifully. The flavor closely resembles the Amarone from Dal Forno, which is similarly made from dried grapes, but costs upwards of 300 bucks. On the finish, it is almost like someone poured molten licorice into the glass.

Dutschke, Sun-Raisined Shiraz; $45/375 ml
Barossa Valley, South Australia
Grapes: Shiraz
18% ABV
300 cases produced
www.dutschkewines.com

This is certainly one of the wines on the list that is almost singular in its approach. With the addition of this wine, the list would more appropriately be titled *Gary Vaynerchuk's 100 Wines and One Syrupy, Sugary, Explosive Beverage That Will Change Your Life.* So, you see why I had to put this in here. It might be a little much, a little Paris Hiltonesque, but I think the epicurean excursion this wine offers is worth the price and the shock therapy it's going to perform on your palate. And, with the potent alcohol and flavors of this wine, you are going to need about ten daring friends just to get through this little bottle, so there is some real value here as well. This stuff is coming way out of left field, and that is precisely the sort of wine you should be excited to experience, even if you choose to drip it over your pancakes and ice cream in order to enjoy it.

Palate Primer:

Soy Sauce

Traditionally made by fermenting soybeans with yeast and koji mold, soy sauce is of Chinese origin and is known for its salty, earthy, savory flavor. Soy sauce is frequently cited as an excellent example of the "fifth taste," known in Japan as *umami*—a characteristic it shares with mushrooms, cheese, and some wines.

INITIAL IMPRESSIONS

This winery first grabbed my attention because its initials are TV, like those of my mother, Tamara Vaynerchuk. Is that a classic Russian name or what? Obviously this list, this book, and my entire life would not exist without her, so this is a great opportunity to thank my mom for giving birth to me. It was my mom who put together the blueprint for all my radness and awesomeness, so a shout-out to my favorite little mommy: I love you. However, even if this winery had the initials TB, which I equate with Tom Brady (who, as a Jets fan, I hate), it would still make the list. Shout-out to Tom Brady: Hey man, I *really* don't like you.

On the nose this wine hits me with major gooseberry and an almost herbal tea component, like silver needle or oolong. There are secondary aromas of pear and a little flinty action that really reminds me of Chablis or Sancerre. This wine is extraordinary on the palate, with a huge, massive, explosive fruit profile dominated by pear, and also bits of kiwi and hints of papaya as it moves to the finish. The mouthfeel is just unparalleled, with

Label Lore

Topanga is taken from the Native American Chumash word meaning "where the ocean meets the mountains." Topanga Vineyards was conceived in the Topanga Canyon in California, where the ocean meets the mountains.

**Topanga Vineyards, Grenache Blanc "Celadon,"
2006; $28**

Clarksburg, California
Grape: Grenache Gris
14.5% ABV
250 cases produced
www.tvwinery.com

the heavy weight of a great Chardonnay, like a Corton-Charlemagne, followed by the razor-sharp acidity of a New Zealand Sauvignon Blanc.

This wine reminds me of some of the cult classic wines that are using Rhône varieties in California, like Sine Qua Non and other wines that command big dollars. I think this wine would totally Buster Douglas many of those wines. Being made from Grenache Blanc, I think this wine has the potential to do something revolutionary. It is probably one of fewer than six examples of this varietal wine in California, and it should really make us all wonder why people are not planting this instead of sticking more crappy Sauvignon Blanc out there. I am totally shocked at how good this wine is.

Grenache Blanc is probably not even in the top ten grapes that most wine drinkers are shopping for, but if you're an adventurer, and you're a little Teddy Roosevelt at heart, you need to find this amazing wine. I applaud this effort because it has the potential to change the wine world.

VAYNERCABULARY

Buster Douglas (v)—*to unexpectedly destroy. Taken from James "Buster" Douglas, the former undisputed world heavyweight boxing champion who knocked out undefeated champion Mike Tyson on February 11, 1990, in Tokyo, Japan.*

THE SOUTH RISES

America has its breadbasket and France has its wine bucket. The south of France, bordering the Mediterranean, is traditionally the source for Vin de Pays and Vin de Table, low-budget and low-impact wines that quench a nation of wine lovers. (Did you think the French drink Châteauneuf-du-Pape over lunch?)

In recent years, producers here have started to plant better-quality grapes, pursuing the "less but better" trend that defines up-and-comer wine regions. Still, Côtes du Roussillon attracts mainly bargain hunters searching for wines priced in the teens, perhaps 20 bucks tops. So, at $40 per bottle, this wine from Domaine Gauby is downright expensive. However, Gauby is a small family estate that is a huge leader in quality. With access to 100-year-old Carignan and Grenache vines and their embrace of biodynamic farming, Gauby cultivated a cultlike following in France. Despite being in the low-rent part of town, demand for Gauby's wines far exceeds the supply, making them like a first-growth from the wrong side of the tracks.

This red, blended from the region's classic grapes, is very tight on the nose, but manages to show some of that rustic character that defines the Languedoc-Roussillon. The plum flavors are really pleasant and obvious, but mixed in are some classic dried meats, like plums wrapped in prosciutto. There is also some tasty black pepper, along with little hints of jalapeño. The nose is slowly opening on this wine, and because it's quite dense, I recommend that you open this at least

Domaine Gauby, Vieilles Vignes Rouge, 2004; $40
AOC Côtes du Roussillon-Villages, France
Grapes: Grenache (45%), Carignan (30%),
    Syrah and Mourvèdre (25%)
12.5% ABV
300 cases produced

two to three hours before drinking.

On the palate, this is really earthy, with fresh fruit and the meaty flavors of venison. It is honest and genuine, and really represents a great value, despite being much pricier than its neighbors. This wine will easily last for five to ten years in the cellar. I desperately want you to try this, because it shows the great potential of not just Gauby, but an entire region.

Meet the Grape:
Carignan

This workhorse grape is the most widely planted red grape in France, valued for its high yields and tolerance for heat. While Carignan generally produces uninteresting wines, by limiting yields and utilizing old vine fruit, talented producers manage to create distinctive wines. Wines of AOC Côtes du Roussillon-Villages may not include more than 60 percent Carignan in the blend.

LIVING UP TO THE LEGEND

Have you ever eaten humble pie? Sit back while I prepare to cut myself a big slice. There is probably no Champagne brand with better marketing hype than one named after a monk who allegedly invented the drink, took a sip, and declared he saw stars. This is the stuff that makes marketers tremble with excitement.

Admittedly, I have called out many of the big Champagne houses and the American suckers that patronize them in this very book. Probably more than anyone, I enjoy taking my jabs at Moët, Clicquot, Perrier-Jouët, Cristal, and Dom P. I go around shooting my mouth off about their outrageous ad spends and escalating prices all the time. This effort, however, is truly magnificent.

This vintage Champagne offers a lot of apple and pear fruit, with a nice rhubarb component on the tail end that really fascinates me. But perhaps what I love most is the big handful of nuts—walnuts, cashews, and almonds. Something about that apple-and-nut combination just blows me away. Add to those flavors the incredible raciness of this wine (yes, I called it wine; Champagne is wine) and you have a spectacular, palate-rousing drink that totally wakes me up. On the finish, there are beautiful yeasty flavors, like walking past Sullivan Street Bakery. This wine is focused, knows what it wants to be, and delivers fruit, nuts, bread—all tied together perfectly. If you've been avoiding Dom Pérignon, maybe even on my advice, it's time to board the monk train. This rivals many of the prior vintages, including the 1990, which was awesome.

When people go to critique this list—and they will, because that's what wine people do—they will probably say there are too many sparkling wines and dessert wines. But this list is not about you listening to me or anyone else. I want you to look to yourself. That's exactly what I do, and right now I happen to be enjoying a lot of bubbles. I want this to be a tool for many people, but it's still a snapshot of my palate right now.

Honestly, I never would have thought this wine would make the list. But to leave it off just because it has a great story and is marketed really well would make me a hypocrite of the worst sort. Pour me another glass of Dom P., and please, pass the pie.

Science Experiment:	Another Bubble

In order to estimate the number of bubbles in your Champagne, simply follow the system of scientist Bill Lembeck: Establish the pressure in the bottle in atmospheres (5.5 at 20°C) and calculate the volume of gas per bottle (252 cubic inches). Next, determine the size of the average bubble (.02 inches) and compute the volume of the sphere (4.2 millionths of a cubic inch). After accounting for gas left in solution, divide the available gas by gas per bubble for the number of bubbles: 49 million.

THINKING MAN'S BORDEAUX

wine country

The relatively small appellation of Pomerol is located on the right bank of the Gironde River in Bordeaux and is planted mostly with Merlot, followed by Cabernet Franc and Cabernet Sauvignon. Unlike other areas of Bordeaux, there has never been a formal classification of the Châteaux in Pomerol, but several famous estates reside here, including Le Pin and Pétrus.

I've established with this list that there are plenty of delicious wines you can pop and enjoy without thinking about anything more serious than a *Love Boat* rerun. However, there are also wines that require thought and introspection—more like a *Fantasy Island* rerun. Tasting this wine took me backwards, forwards, and in circles. I like to call it a crossword puzzle wine, because it requires concentration. Make your tasting notes in pencil.

The big, brawny Pomerols of 2005 are rolling out with some hefty prices. They are great wines for the serious Bordeaux fans: the thinkers and the collectors. Those of you who are just looking for some good wine to drink may want to pass on this, because it will totally out-dork you. Even I hate to be out-dorked.

This wine is outright monstrous, with massive charcoal and cassis flavors. There is this old-school candy flavor, like grape candy, blackberry, and licorice rolled together. I also get some secondary bacon fat, and this enormous heft to the mouthfeel. There is also some Starbucks coffee and hot chocolate on the finish. It's like chomping

Château La Clémence, 2005; $110
AOC Pomerol, Bordeaux, France
Grapes: Merlot (85%), Cabernet Franc (15%)
14% ABV
500 cases produced
www.vignobles-dauriac.com
www.bobbofman.com

on grape candy and then chasing it down with a cup of that fancy, boutique, single-estate hot chocolate.

This wine reminds me of some of the great 1982 Pomerols that I enjoyed so much. It has the structure, the elegance, and the backbone to last for fifteen years easily. And these really complex secondary flavors will keep even an experienced taster guessing for a few hours. This is no pizza wine. When you are ready to get serious about tasting wine, put on some jazz and go get Zen by the fireplace: This is the stuff you want in your glass. Tasting this wine, trying to figure out what it was saying, was a struggle for me. And sometimes that's exactly the challenge a dedicated wine lover is looking for.

Palate Primer:

Bacon Fat

In the U.S., bacon is made primarily from smoked, sliced pork belly and is consistently about 50 percent fat to actual meat. Bacon can also be made from a wide variety of pork cuts, including the back. It is typically richly flavored with wood smoke and salt.

#11 PUZZLE IN A GLASS

wine country

The most northerly appellation in the Languedoc, Pic Saint-Loup lies nearly 20 miles from the Mediterranean in the foothills of the Cévennes. The quality red grapes planted here include Syrah, Grenache, and Mourvèdre. Red wine designated Pic Saint-Loup must include two of the three. In addition, Carignan and Cinsault can be used, but not for more than 10 percent of the finished wine. Rosé wines are also permitted. www.pic-saint-loup.com

I've told you more than once how educational it can be to go back and retaste the same wine every six months, taking notes about how the wine, and your own palate, have changed over time. Well, let me introduce you to a wine that is part of my personal game plan for the next three years. I have been drinking a lot of wine from the Languedoc, but perhaps none is more compelling and perplexing to me than this wine. Each time I thought I had this wine figured out, it changed in my glass. This wine is like catching a tiger by the tail. And when a wine takes me to that world, you know I'll be back for more.

With a fascinating aroma of fresh basil meets goji berry, this Grenache-Syrah blend is an exotic mix of West meets East, reminding me of California cuisine and also China. In the flavor, there is some mulberry, leading to a great sour cherry finish, which is also a little stinky and dirty, like an escargot mud pie. The mid-palate is so meaty, it is like drinking steak. Remember that classic SNL skit about the Bass-o-matic? This wine is the Buffal-o-matic, like gamy buffalo meat in a blender, along with some stunning fruit that is interesting and structured.

This wine is drinking well right now, but given its structure and complexity, I predict it will last for three to five years. I have not been this perplexed since tenth-grade science class and the periodic table of the elements. This wine is really a conundrum, and exactly the type of challenge that a wine lover can have fun with for years. It's slightly pricier than a crossword book, but this wine will open your world to new flavors, as well as the great potential of Languedoc. So find a wine that baffles you, buy a bunch, and enjoy the challenge.

Palate Primer:

Buffalo

The American Bison, while not a true buffalo, frequently goes by this name. Bison meat is very lean, with less fat and fewer calories than skinless chicken. It is high in iron and other nutrients, and has 40 percent more protein than beef. If you have not tasted bison recently, it may be because, according to the National Bison Association, there are only 150,000 bison total in the U.S., compared to the 124,000 cattle slaughtered daily.

#10

A MONUMENTAL WINE FROM WASHINGTON

The 2003 Boudreaux Cab is one of the highest-rated wines in the history of WLTV. And this outrageously good 2004, hot on its heels, confirms my suspicions: First, winemaker Rob Newsom is a relative newcomer, but an amazing talent. And second, Washington State is on its way to becoming the premier red wine–producing state in America. There. I said it. I think Washington wineries have the temperament, the thought process, the focus, the *terroir*, and the hunger necessary to become the best red wine state. I see this wine as a catalyst and Rob Newsom as a torchbearer, because they are making some of America's best wines that are also great values.

This wine reminds me of some of the astounding Washington Cabs I've had from Quilceda Creek and Leonetti Cellars, which is not surprising since Newsom hatched his plan over a bottle of Leonetti with founder and friend Gary Figgins. This Boudreaux Cab is loaded with dark cherries and chocolate mint, like some exotic dessert in a five-

Label Lore

Gary Figgins and son Chris bestowed on Rob Newsom the nickname "Boudreaux" after a popular folklore character from Newsom's native Louisiana. As the protagonist in local stories and jokes, Boudreaux is loved for his sense of adventure and good humor. Newsom's first wine, a 1998 Merlot Cabernet Franc blend, was dubbed The Cru Boudreaux.

wine country

Washington is the nation's second largest wine-producing state, with over 30,000 acres under vine and more than 530 wineries in operation. More than twenty wine grape varieties are grown there—about 56 percent white and 44 percent red, the latter led by Merlot, Cabernet Sauvignon, and Syrah.

star restaurant. The flavors are rich and powerful on the mid-palate, with just so much complexity—cedar box, hints of leather, and fine levels of dirt. Take all these flavors, imagine squeezing a ripe orange on top, and that is this wine.

When I sit down to my finest steak dinner of the year—a nice aged rib eye maybe—this is the one wine in this book I would most like to have at my side. I really can't think of a bigger compliment than that. This is a tour de force, a humbling experience for a wine drinker, and will last thirteen to fifteen years. You know how crazy I am about Bordeaux, but they have nothing on Boudreaux, because this is one of my favorite Cabernets from anywhere. This Cab has me totally excited about what's to come from Washington and especially from this small, literally off-the-grid winery in the Cascade Mountains.

ZINFANDEL AND COMPANY

The grape list for this wine looks like some sort of high school trigonometry test. That's because the fruit is not blended by the winemaker, but by the guy who planted the vineyard—starting more than 100 years ago. Founded by William McPherson Hill in 1851, it's believed that Zinfandel was growing here as early as 1855. What now exists in the vineyard constitutes a century of little experiments, amounting to what we in the wine world refer to as a field blend. There are at least fourteen different grapes intermingled with the mostly Zinfandel field, making it one of the most fascinating vineyards in California. Since the blend meets the 75 percent minimum requirement, it can be labeled simply as a Zinfandel varietal wine.

When Old Hill Ranch was purchased and revitalized by Otto and Anne Teller in 1981, they got their start selling this same fruit to Joel Peterson at Ravenswood Winery, one of Sonoma's great Zinfandel proponents. But old vine California Zinfandel like this really found appreciation in the 1990s, when wine geeks were practically selling their children to get on the mailing list for Turley Zin.

This is huge, extracted, ripe, monster Zin. On the nose there is a gorgeous concentration of raspberry jam and black cherry soda. It also has some of that Dr. Pepper secret spice, a little white pepper dancing around in there, so this is a big-time soda lover's wine.

The fruit concentration on this wine is so massive that for the

Bucklin, Old Hill Ranch Zinfandel, 2005; $35
Sonoma Valley, California
Grapes: Zinfandel (77%), Grenache (6.8%), Alicante Bouchet
   (6.5%), Petite Sirah (2.1%), Mourvèdre (1.3%), Grand Noir (1.3%),
   Tannat (1%), Carignan (.6%), Lenoir (.3%), Trousseau (.3%)
15.6% ABV
766 cases produced
www.buckzin.com

first second I hate it, but I quickly get over it. There is some Hi-C fruit punch fakeness, but the new oak is so creamy and integrated just perfectly. The flavor reminds me of a great pastry shop in Paris, with fresh cream and raspberry sauce. Or, if you don't frequent a lot of Paris patisseries, just imagine IHOP raspberry pancake syrup. This wine is fairly booming with fruit, along with nice spiciness and a red pepper component on the finish. It is one of the nicest representations of the Zinfandel grape I've come across all year (and my highest-ranked American wine), even if it did have help from a few friends.

Meet the Grape:
Zinfandel

Zinfandel is the second-most planted grape in California: the grape more associated with America than any other. It can produce a variety of wines, from intense high-alcohol reds to sweet blush "white Zinfandel." Genetic testing has proved a common ancestry with the Primitivo grape of Italy and Crljenak Kaštelanski, a Croatian variety.

#8 TINY BUBBLES

I'll admit that P. Diddy may know a lot about music and fashion, but I encourage you to get your Champagne advice elsewhere. Sure, this Champagne may not have a familiar name that flows effortlessly into rap lyrics or a yellow cellophane wrapper, but I would rather drink it than Dom P. or Cristal any day. Champagne is actually an unexplored wine category for most people, because Clicquot and Moët and Perrier-Jouët have all the marketing dollars and all the sales. There are about a hundred Champagne houses and thousands of small growers, but the twenty biggest houses account for about one-third of sales.

The nose of this wine is just tremendously exciting, with a yeasty, bready component and some fresh pear peel. It has apples for days! In order to replicate this aroma, you would have to go to the orchard, pick ten kinds of apples—from Red Delicious to Granny Smith—and take them home and juice them together. There are also some subtle almonds, along with almond shells, fresh baguette, and subtle hints of margarine and butter. It's not oaky in the sense of an oak monster, buttery Chardonnay; there is just a touch. It's far fresher, more like an oak tree with handfuls of fresh green leaves.

The name of this Champagne means "between the sky and earth," which is very much where these vines live, breathe, and produce. This wine was the first modern Champagne made from grapes grown without the use of fertilizers or chemicals, and the Bedel estate, an

**Françoise Bedel, Champagne Brut
"Entre Ciel et Terre," NV; $70**

AOC Champagne, France
Grapes: Chardonnay (41%), Pinot Noir (35%), Pinot Meunier (24%)
12% ABV
100 cases imported
www.champagne-francoise-bedel.fr
www.johndavidwine.com

area of only about seventeen acres, is now farmed entirely biodynamically.

Before you grab the familiar yellow label, overpriced prestige cuvée, or bulk-produced Champagne, take a closer look at the small producers. The smallest thirty Champagne houses produce only 5 percent of the Champagne, so it may take some searching, but my top ten would not be complete without some serious boutique bubbles. Only 600 cases of this wine are made for the world, and it is obnoxiously complex, with an amazing mid-palate and a long finish. Very crisp, very clean, very true. It is just insanely over-the-top good! And since Jay-Z is feuding with Cristal, you may want to find this Champagne before he finds a word that rhymes with "Bedel."

Meet the Grape:
Pinot Meunier

A mutation of Pinot Noir, Pinot Meunier is a red grape and one of only three grapes authorized for use in Champagne. It's said to contribute acidity to the final wine, and the variety's tendency to bud late and ripen early makes it well suited for colder climates like that of Champagne.

ONE MORE FROM THE LOIRE

When I think about what I love about wine—things like finding a total gem from some little place that will totally light up a summer day—well, this is the stuff! This wine has honey-covered baby apples galore! Actually, it's almost more like apple candy, this candy in the 1980s called Appleheads that was in a container that looked like juice and would say "contains real apple juice" even though it was like one drop per million boxes. It has that really intense artificial apple smell more than it has pure fresh apple on the aroma. It is just beautiful and clean and there are tons and tons of minerals. It smells like there was a cracked sidewalk, with all the stones breaking out, and someone came along with ten apples and just started smashing them on that sidewalk.

On the palate there is a very pretty apple and pear component. For a split second, I felt like there was residual sugar, some sweetness, but really there is *none* at all. The fruit is just so pure, so delicious,

---

VAYNERCABULARY

NW (n)—Nantucket Wine. There are vineyards planted on this vacation island off the coast of Massachusetts, but Nantucket Wines refers not so much to wines that are from Nantucket as those that should be there with you—particularly seafood-friendly whites.

that it seems like sugar coming through. Now, that's when you know the fruit is completely pure. This wine is very clean, very crisp— it's really making me yearn for oysters and crab cakes right now.

It's not exactly inexpensive at almost $23, but it is one of the most affordable wines to crack my top ten. I realize a lot of Americans might hesitate to spend that money, especially for Chenin Blanc, especially from this obscure, peculiar little place in the Loire Valley called Jasnières. But when I think about wines that I want to consume in the summer, mostly with shellfish, this is it, a total NW— Nantucket Wine. If I'm on the beach, enjoying great seaside food or a clambake, then this is the wine that I want! It's an amazing, clean expression of white wine that will harmonize with your food, but it has great appeal and plenty of complexity to appease the red wine drinkers in the crowd.

Palate Primer:

Appleheads

Appleheads are bite-size hard candies made by Ferrara Pan of Chicago, the manufacturers of Lemonheads. The name was formerly Johnny Apple Treats. Likewise, Grapeheads were previously called Alexander the Grape and Cherryheads were once named Cherry Clan. www.ferrarapan.com

#6

A LEBANESE CONTENDER

Every now and then I am shotgunning through wines and something stops me dead in my tracks. This wine from Lebanon recently blindsided me, and retasting it now, I think it may be one of the most eye-opening wines I encountered while assembling this list.

This winery debuted in Lebanon in 1999, a fairly new venture considering the family has been distilling Arak there since 1893. Arak is an anise-flavored liquor that most Americans probably would not drink on a dare, but don't let that deter you. According to the family, Domaine Wardy captured 10 percent of the Lebanese wine market within two years, and after tasting this, I can clearly see why.

This is Wardy's top bottle, made from grapes grown in Lebanon's highest-altitude vineyards, so it's not inexpensive. But the aroma . . .

Palate Primer:

Splenda

Introduced in 1999, Splenda is a brand of the noncaloric, artificial sweetener sucralose. The sweetener begins with sugar and alters it by selectively replacing three hydrogen-oxygen groups on the sugar molecule with three chlorine atoms. The resulting sweetener is 600 times sweeter than regular table sugar, twice as sweet as saccharin, and four times as sweet as aspartame.

Domaine Wardy, Private Selection, 2006; $80

Bekaa Valley, Lebanon
Grapes: Syrah (33%), Cabernet Sauvignon (33%), Merlot (33%)
15% ABV
800 cases imported
www.domaine-wardy.com
www.bobbofman.com

it is obnoxious with marmalade and mandarin. It's almost like being in a spa, like I got locked in the mall after hours and I'm in the Body Shop in the dark fumbling through the oils and gels and creams. It is just so tropical, with enormous amounts of explosive raspberry and orange. It's actually very citrusy, with a mix of oranges, mandarin, and tangerine that become almost oily on the nose.

This wine is very New World in style, with its big fruit and inky color. The flavor is just loaded with candy. This is a free-for-all at the five-and-dime. Someone put the whole penny candy counter into a piñata and I just smashed the hell out of it. Mixed in with that is all this extremely powerful, massively complex black fruit—blueberries, blackberries, and black currants. While this is very New World, very candied, I do not want to give the impression it is all syrupy-sweet-Splenda-fake sugar. It's the sort of Mike-Tyson-in-his-prime left-hook-to-your-jaw fruit punch that I can really get behind. It's executed with elegance and impact! *Pow!* I'd love for Old World fans to experience this because it has some real structure and depth behind all that fruit. Honestly, you'll probably hate on it anyway. But won't you give it a try? For me?

KEEPING IT REAL IN FRIULI

If you could see this wine now, you would be saying, "This is seriously weird shit!" The color of this wine is like aging copper. In fact, I sometimes call it the "penny wine." It is definitely not a color that would encourage many white wine fans to put this in their mouths; it looks more like battery acid or apple cider than wine. And, if you look closely at the vintage, you'll see the current release is from 2002, so you know already this guy is on a totally different page.

"This guy" is Stanko Radikon. He practices winemaking much the way his grandfather did in the 1930s. The grape blend for this wine is a field blend, which means that the grapes are actually planted interspersed throughout the vineyard. It's like a mixed bag of jelly beans—you grab a handful and take what you get. Radikon also does not use conventional winemaking practices like adding yeast or sulphur, all of which amount to this wine being real. I can't think of a better description or a bigger compliment than to say this wine is *real*.

In some respects, the color is reflected in the smell: There is

Label Lore

When you see just the word "Sauvignon" on a traditional Italian wine label, it refers to the Sauvignon Blanc grape as opposed to Cabernet Sauvignon. Sauvignon is planted mostly in northeast Italy, but is occasionally found as far south as Tuscany and Piedmont.

Radikon, Oslavje, 2002; $43
IGT Friuli, Italy
Grapes: Chardonnay (40%), Pinot Grigio (30%), Sauvignon (30%)
13.5% ABV
1,000 cases imported

almost a rusty nail aroma, which is followed by some spoiled papaya. Not sold? You throw some rusty nails and papaya in my mouth and I'm excited. On the palate, it has some petrol and smushed pea flavors, along with a potent element of red radish, and a little bit of that pineapple juice—the canned stuff that covers the rings. There is just something about this wine that is so genuine, so fresh, so vibrant—and so very real. It's like that one kid in high school who really knows who he is and marches to his own beat.

This wine also has a really long finish, which you know I love, and it would be especially great with food. In fact, Radikon has started bottling it in 500 ml bottles because he believes it is a more food-friendly size. With half-liter bottles, a couple can have a white and a red over dinner—and you know sharing wine with people is what I'm all about. If you are a little bit daring, a fan of whole fish with all the bones, like a baked branzino, this wine is a great match and the perfect wine for you. My top five wines would not be complete without something this original, unexpected, and outrageous.

#4 JEWISH BORDEAUX

More than any other wine, this is the wine I am writing this book for. Read the label: "Special Reserve, Kosher for Passover, made in Israel." On paper, there are not a lot of selling points for this wine. And, it costs $60. Practically no one is interested in buying this wine. That's because people who drop 60 bones on a bottle of wine do not normally do it in the Kosher aisle. After all, we all know that Kosher wine comes in a jug and is nothing more than SJJ (that's sweet junk juice).

I'm here to persuade you otherwise. This wine smells like nothing less than a classic Right Bank Bordeaux from a great vintage. I've had it open for several hours, and not only does it smell like $60, it smells more like $70 or $80. It's only getting better. First, it has beautiful, dark cassis, very polished vanilla, and some maple tree bark on the nose. It's almost popping with dark cherry fruit. Everything is so integrated— the oak, the vanilla, the fruit. This wine was painted by a master, every stroke in the right place.

The mouthfeel alone on this wine is worth the $60. It's elegant

> ### Label Lore
>
> Not all Israeli wine is Kosher, and not all Kosher wine is Israeli. "Kosher" does not indicate a wine's style or quality, but refers to wines that have been certified to follow Jewish dietary laws. For example, Kosher wine is handled only by Sabbath-observant Jews and made only from vineyards that are at least four years old.

Tishbi Estate Winery, Jonathan Tishbi Special Reserve Sde Boker Vineyard, 2004; $60

Negev, Israel

Grapes: Cabernet Sauvignon (50%), Merlot (40%), Cabernet Franc (10%)

14% ABV

300 cases imported

www.tishbi.com

wine country

Wine has been produced in Israel since biblical times, nearly 2,000 years before Europe. The nation is now widely planted with international grape varieties and includes these wine-growing regions: Galil (Galilee), Judean Hills, Shimshon (Samson), Negev, Sharon, and Golan Heights.

and polished, and the tannins are so beautifully integrated. Now, here's where I get excited: In the secondary flavors, there is a very distinctive flavor of pomegranate that is just exuberant, along with licorice and black chocolate flavors. This wine is tight, tannic, explosive, and made to last.

Here's my fantasy for this wine. I want to gather thirty master sommeliers. What the heck—let's all meet in Vegas. We'll have a blast, and they all live there now anyway. Then, I would blind taste this wine with them against 2003 Bordeaux. I'm telling you that in a tasting of $60 to $100 retail Bordeaux, this wine will be in the top quarter. I am glowing over how good this is. It is absolutely one of the top Kosher wines I've ever come across, but I would honestly recommend this no matter where it came from, which is why it clocks in at number four on this list. This is the perfect example of why your preconceived notions need to go out the door.

CHILE THROUGH THE LOOKING GLASS

The second I smelled this wine I knew it was going to come in near the top of this list—and sure enough, it made the winning trifecta. This is absolutely one of the most exciting white wines I've tasted in a really long time. It reminds me of the revelation I had circa 1996, when I first came across Cloudy Bay Sauvignon Blanc from New Zealand. I knew I was tasting something fundamentally different—something that could change the way not just I, but an entire generation, thought about wine. I see that potential in this wine.

This wine has just cemented a prediction I've been thinking about for a while: Chile will be known for its Sauvignon Blanc above anything else. The reason: This wine brings $40 super-Sancerre value for under 14 bones.

First, I can't get over this extraordinary smell of menthol and pine needles. It's like getting lost in a forest in Washington State. The fresh pine is so intense it's almost like Mr. Clean. If it wasn't so deli-

Science Experiment:	Smell the Glass
Sometimes a wine's aromas are easier to detect after you empty the glass, and this wine is a great example. If you don't smell the string bean and pine at first, smell the emptied glass. The increased surface area and warming effect on the glass can make aromas more apparent.	

Luis Felipe Edwards, Gran Reserva Sauvignon Blanc, 2007; $14

Leyda Valley, Chile
Grape: Sauvignon Blanc
13.5% ABV
3,000 cases imported

cious you'd want to scrub your kitchen floor with it. There is also freshly cut grass, like the person in your neighborhood with the nicest green lawn just cut it on a cool fall day, picked up a handful, and held it to your face. There is also a very serious string bean component. It has the enormous grassy component, the stuff we all love in New Zealand Sauvignon Blanc, but that extra pine kick is just completely seducing me.

The flavor just explodes in the mouth. It's like an Atari 2600 Kaboom! bomb that takes out all your taste buds with its huge gooseberry flavor. It really does its job—explosive, but with polish, elegance, and perfect acidity. And on the finish, it is almost cucumber-esque, like cucumbers with a little bit of sugar.

This wine is why I love the wine industry. This is seriously life-changing stuff for 14 bucks. When the word gets out on this, it could get real scary with people running around like it's 1984 and they are clubbing the other moms to get a Cabbage Patch Kid. Please, don't do that. But do find this wine.

YOUTH AND BEAUTY

This wine could have been my number one wine of the year for many reasons. First, it is one of the greatest cedar box-cassis-blackberry-black currant wines I've come across in my life. It has a handful of Goobers in the mid-palate, so it's like going to the movies and instead of slurping a $10 bucket of soda, enjoying one of the best bottles of wine you've ever tasted.

There is one problem that holds it back: This wine is expensive. Despite how amazing this wine is, it is seriously tough for me to stomach paying $250 for a bottle of wine. The ironic thing is that even at 250 bones, this wine offers value. I have been fortunate enough to sample the first-growth Bordeaux for about the past eight years now. And in 2005, these names—like Lafite-Rothschild, Latour, and Margaux—are all bringing $400, $500, even $600 a bottle. Well, I have tasted this second-growth 2005 multiple times and it is right there with, if not better than, many of the top names.

Label Lore

Deuxièmes Cru, or "Second Growth," is one of the official classifications of Bordeaux's Médoc Châteaux established in 1855. The classification included fifteen Châteaux whose quality was considered second only to the First Growths. Château Mouton Rothschild is the only Château to have ascended from Second Growth to First, in 1973.

Château Cos d'Estournel, 2005; $250

Deuxièmes Cru, AOC Saint-Estèphe, Bordeaux, France

Grapes: Cabernet Sauvignon (78%), Merlot (19%), Cabernet Franc (3%)

13.5% ABV

Less than 16,000 cases produced

www.cosestournel.com

www.bobbofman.com

Given a great vintage opportunity, it's obvious to me that these guys put everything they had into this wine. This is a Hulk Hogan vs. Iron Sheik scale effort. While Cos d'Estournel has long been a respected contender, they should be proud that this wine will take on the very best of a stellar vintage and win.

Of course, all wine lovers are cursed with 20/20 hindsight, and it breaks my heart that this wine sold for just $60 about eight years ago and now commands $250. However, I have been fortunate enough to taste it, and I am hoping some of you will make the splurge. Hey, this is what the market dictates. Coffee is $4 a cup now, so quit busting my balls. I promise you, this is the most cost-effective way to taste the best of the vintage.

You could certainly drink this wine soon. It is one of the best young Bordeaux wines I have ever tasted, and I think with some decanting you could fully enjoy this within the next three years. Of course, I am too young to have tasted the 1982s at this stage, but nothing in the much-touted 2000 vintage came close. However, this wine will be at its best with twenty-five years in the cellar, waiting for your most special celebration. For me, it might be a Jets Super Bowl victory. Let's hope I don't have to wait that long.

#1 JUST DESSERTS

A t the start of this list, I pledged that no wine would be excluded from consideration. That approach has paid off: the other 100 wines are from mega- producers, dedicated entrepreneurs, and family farms alike. We've traversed continents to explore wine country in Spain and Chile, California and Israel. And we've tasted wine grapes ranging from the overexposed (Pinot Grigio) to the obscure (Sagrantino). This feels a little like preparing for a final exam, when you look back at your notes and think, "Wow, we covered a lot of ground here." But even if you don't remember the details, I hope you'll agree that there has never been a better time to be a wine lover.

As difficult as the decision is, only one wine can occupy the top spot as my most exciting. In some ways, this wine is predictable. After all, it is French, and their wines are the model for wine production around the world. However, this is also a dessert wine, which even I never could have predicted at the outset. Frankly, this wine is better than most of the Château d'Yquem I've tasted. That's not a total surprise to me, considering that if you go back close to a century, Doisy-Védrines sold for *more* than Château d'Yquem—which is without a doubt the most famous name in Sauternes.

DV has a killer pedigree as a legendary producer and a top-quality estate, and I'm a longtime fan. Sure, there have been vintages I have not loved as much as others, but let's talk specifically about 2005.

Château Doisy-Védrines, Sauternes, 2005; $39
AOC Barsac, France
Grapes: Sémillon (80%), Sauvignon Blanc (17%), Muscadelle (3%)
14% ABV
500 cases imported
www.bobbofman.com

This vintage was nothing less than spectacular in Bordeaux. And in Sauternes, in particular, it may be one of the greatest vintages of all time! When these wines hit the market, and word on this book gets out, they are going to be devoured by dessert wine lovers like Pac-Man gobbling up dots. You'll need to act fast.

The aroma of this wine is incredibly bright, with beautiful sweet honey, and an almost cashew, peanutlike component. If you ever wondered what lemon-covered pineapple would smell like, this is it. All I can say is—wow! This has such an elegant, gorgeous nose, it is almost like being introduced to royalty. From the first handshake, you know you are dealing with a different league of class, breeding, and grace.

The flavor is just stupid good! It is shocking to me that there is a wine that can taste like this. It is so elegant, with an extraordinary mouthfeel—so polished and clean. I feel like there is a waterfall of flavors pouring into my mouth, including papaya, guava, and here comes that guy in a barrel . . . but wait—it's actually a barrel full of lemons! This wine is never viscous or heavy; it's just flavorful, balanced, and elegant. And while this wine is not inexpensive, it's certainly not out of reach for one of the great vintages of one of the world's greatest dessert wine regions. This may be one of the best values in Sauternes I've come across in my life. And despite some serious competition, it is undoubtedly the most exciting wine I've tasted this year.

Looking for Thunderful wines to suit a specific meal, taste, or occasion?

Try these recommendations from Gary.

BEST WITH
CANDLES AND BARRY WHITE

Arista
Russian River Valley Pinot Noir
2005

Hess Collection
Cabernet Sauvignon
2005

J Vineyards & Winery
Cuvée 20
NV

Slowine
Rosé
2007

Moët & Chandon
Dom Pérignon Vintage
1999

BEST FOR
GIFT-GIVING

Luis Felipe Edwards
Gran Reserva Sauvignon Blanc
2007

De Conciliis
Selim Spumante
NV

Hess Collection
Cabernet Sauvignon
2005

Paso Creek
Merlot
2005

Château Beaumont Haut-Médoc
2004

BEST WITH
STEAK

Boudreaux Cellars
Cabernet Sauvignon
2004

Cyclo
Christina
2005

Caracol Serrano
Tinto Joven
2005

Domaine du Banneret
Châteauneuf-du-Pape
2005

Hess Collection
Mount Veeder Cabernet Sauvignon
2005

Ojai
Pinot Noir Clos Pepe Vineyard
2005

Ascheri
Montalupa Langhe Viognier
2004

Bodegas el Nido
Clio
2006

Bartolomeo
Barolo
2004

Château Valrose
Cuvée Alienor
2004

BEST WITH
SEAFOOD

Bénédicte de Rycke
Jasnières, Cuvée Louise
2005

Monarchia Winery
Battonage Chardonnay
2006

Moondarra Vineyard
Holly's Garden Pinot Gris
2006

Danubio
Grüner Veltliner
2006

Domaine du Banneret
Châteauneuf-du-Pape
2005

BEST WITH
PIZZA

Fairvalley
Pinotage
2006

Caracol Serrano
Tinto Joven
2005

Bodegas Berberana S.A.
Berberano Numero Uno Tempranillo
2005

Ascheri
Barolo Vigna dei Pola
2003

Dievole
Chianti Classico Riserva Novecento
2004

BEST FOR
WINE NEWBIES

Montevino
Terre d'Oro Teroldego
2006

Clos Delorme
Valençay
2005

Danubio
Grüner Veltliner
2006

De Conciliis
Selim Spumante
NV

Paso Creek
Merlot
2005

BEST WITH
SOMETHING
YOU SHOT

Clos Marie
Pic Saint-Loup Cuvée Simon
2004

Clos Delorme
Valençay
2005

Caracol Serrano
Tinto Joven
2005

Domaine du Banneret
Châteauneuf-du-Pape
2005

Ojai
Pinot Noir Clos Pepe Vineyard
2005

PROOF YOU'RE
A VAYNIAC

Dutschke
Sun-Raisined Shiraz

Radikon
Oslavje
2002

Lachini Vineyards
Estate Pinot Noir
2005

Clos Marie
Pic Saint-Loup Cuvée Simon
2004

Clos Delorme
Valençay
2005

BEST FOR
THOSE WHO
DOUBT THE THUNDER

Kilikanoon
Covenant Shiraz
2005

Jocelyn Lonen Winery
Napa Valley Cabernet Sauvignon
2005

Ascheri
Barolo Vigna dei Pola
2003

Tishbi Estates
Jonathan Tishbi Special Reserve
2004

Château La Clémence
2005

BEST FOR
A FIRST DATE

Topanga Vineyards
Grenache Blanc Celadon
2006

Slowine
Rosé
2007

Gainey Vineyard
Riesling Santa Ynez Valley
2006

Paso Creek
Merlot
2005

Pirie Tasmania
South Estelle
2006

BEST TO
IMPRESS
THE IN-LAWS

Françoise Bedel
Champagne Brut Entre Ciel et Terra
NV

Château Reignac
Cuvée Balthus
2005

Château Barde-Haut
2005

Hess Collection
Mount Veeder Cabernet Sauvignon
2005

Taylor Fladgate
Quinta de Vargellas
2005

BEST FOR
THANKSGIVING

Fox Gordon
By George
2005

Pirie Tasmania
South Estelle
2006

Lachini Vineyards
Estate Pinot Noir
2005

Gainey Vineyard
Riesling Santa Ynez Valley
2006

Slowine
Rosé
2007

BEST
FATHER'S DAY GIFTS

Boudreaux Cellars
Cabernet Sauvignon
2004

Prats & Symington
Chryseia Douro
2005

Hess Collection
Mount Veeder Cabernet Sauvignon
2005

Château La Fleur de Boüard
2004

Venge
Scouts Honor Red
2005

BEST TO
STICK IN
THE CELLAR

Madonna Alta
Sagrantino di Montefalco
2004

Cyclo
Christina
2005

Cambiata
Estate Bottled Tannat
2005

Château Cos d'Estournel
2005

Taylor Fladgate
Quinta de Vargellas
2005

BEST TO
BLOW YOUR ECONOMIC
STIMULUS CHECK

Château Cos d'Estournel
2005

Moët & Chandon
Dom Pérignon
Vintage
1999

Campagnola
Caterina Zardini
Amarone della Valpolicella Classico
2004

La Gerla
Brunello di Montalcino Riserva
2003

Château La Clémence
2005

MOST
EARTH-FRIENDLY

Françoise Bedel
Champagne Brut Entre Ciel et Terra
NV

Ceàgo Vinegarden
Sauvignon Blanc Kathleen's Vineyard
2006

Domaine Gauby
Vieilles Vignes Rouge
2004

Clos des Moiselles
Le Bordeaux Merlot
2005

Château Maris
La Touge Syrah
2004

Slowine
Rosé
2007

Moondarra Vineyard
Holly's Garden Pinot Gris
2006

WHITES FOR RED DRINKERS

Ascheri
Montalupa Langhe Viognier
2004

Radikon
Oslavje
2002

Rideau Vineyard
In-Circle Cellar Club Estate Viognier
2006

Verget Chablis
Les Clos
2006

Monarchia Winery
Battonage Chardonnay
2006

REDS FOR WHITE DRINKERS

Fairvalley
Pinotage
2006

Maison Louis Jadot Château des Jacques
Clos de Rochegrès
2006

Domaine St-Nicolas Fièfs Vendéens
Pinot Noir Cuvée Jacques
2005

Clos des Moiselles
Le Bordeaux Merlot
2005

Staete Landt Vineyards
Marlborough Pinot Noir
2006

BEST IN PLACE OF
YET ANOTHER
NEW ZEALAND SAUVIGNON BLANC

Topanga Vineyards
Grenache Blanc
Celadon
2006

Alma Rosa
Pinot Blanc La Encantada Vineyard
2005

Gunn Estate
Unoaked Chardonnay
2007

Moondarra Vineyard
Holly's Garden Pinot Gris
2006

Domaine Tselepos
Moschofilero
2006

OUTRAGEOUS
GRAPES

Cambiata
Estate Bottled Tannat
2005 (Tannat)

Madonna Alta
Sagrantino di Montefalco
2004 (Sagrantino)

Montevino
Terre d'Oro Teroldego
2006 (Teroldego)

Rocca Bernarda
Picolit
2005 (Picolit)

Takler
Noir Gold Kékfrankos Reserve
2006 (Kékfrankos)

MOST LIKELY TO
KNOCK YOU OUT
(I.E. HIGHEST ALCOHOL)

Warre's & Co.
Vintage Port
1983

Dutschke
Sun-Raisined Shiraz

Bucklin
Old Hill Ranch Zinfandel
2005

Campagnola
Caterina Zardini Amarone della Valpolicella Classico
2004

Bodegas El Nido
Clio
2006

BEST FOR
OPERATING HEAVY MACHINERY
(I.E. LOWEST ALCOHOL)

Reymos
Espumoso de Moscatel
NV

Selaks
Premium Selection Ice Wine
2006

Rao's
Prosecco VSAQ Extra Dry
NV

Domaine Imperial Hétszölo
Tokaji Aszú 5 Puttonyos
2001

Danubio
Grüner Veltliner
2006

OAK MONSTER ALERT

Nord Estate Wines
Petite Sirah Jonquil Vineyards
2004

Alpha Omega
Proprietary Red Wine
2005

PreVail Mountain Winery
West Face
2004

Massaya
Gold Reserve
2004

Anderson's Conn Valley Vineyards
Napa Valley Cabernet Sauvignon Estate Reserve
2005

BEST FOR OAK-HATERS

Gunn Estate
Unoaked Chardonnay
2007

Domaine Tselepos
Moschofilero
2006

Slowine
Rosé
2007

Gainey Vineyard
Riesling Santa Ynez Valley
2006

Alpha Omega
Sauvignon Blanc
2007

BIGGEST FRUIT BOMBS

Viñedos de Paganos
La Nieta
2006

Bodegas el Nido
Clio
2006

Massaya
Gold Reserve
2004

Alpha Omega
Proprietary Red Wine
2005

Ojai
Pinot Noir Clos Pepe Vineyard
2005

BEST TO WATCH THE JETS OPENER

Bucklin
Old Hill Ranch Zinfandel
2005

Maison Louis Jadot
Château des Jacques, Clos de Rochegrès
2006

Real Companhia Velha
Evel Grand Escolha
2004

Château Beaumont Haut-Médoc
2004

2 Brothers
Cabernet Sauvignon Reserve
2005

MOST AFFORDABLE
REDS

Bodegas Berberana
S.A. Berberano Numero Uno
Tempranillo
2005 ($9)

Caracol Serrano
Tinto Joven
2005 ($9)

Fairvalley
Pinotage
2006 ($10)

Montevino
Terre d'Oro Teroldego
2006 ($13)

Peirano Estate Vineyards
The Other
2006 ($13)

MOST AFFORDABLE
WHITES

Danubio
Grüner Veltliner
2006 ($13)

Luis Felipe Edwards
Gran Reserva Sauvignon Blanc
2007 ($14)

Gainey Vineyard
Riesling Santa Ynez Valley
2006 ($14)

Gunn Estate Unoaked Chardonnay
2007 ($16)

Pirie Tasmania
South Estelle
2006 ($17)

Domaine St-Nicolas Fièfs Vendéens
Pinot Noir Cuvée Jacques
2005

Bénédicte de Rycke
Jasnières Cuvée Louise
2005

Rao's
Prosecco VSAQ Extra Dry
NV

Gainey Vineyard
Riesling Santa Ynez Valley
2006

Domaine Tselepos
Moschofilero
2006

BEST FROM
PLACES YOU LEAST EXPECTED

Tishbi Estates
Jonathan Tishbi Special Reserve
2004 (Israel)

Domaine Wardy
Private Selection
2006 (Lebanon)

Domaine Tselepos
Moschofilero
2006 (Greece)

Domaine Imperial Hétszölo
Tokaji Aszú 5 Puttonyos
2001 (Hungary)

Prats & Symington Lda
Chryseia Douro
2005 (Portugal)

MOST EXPENSIVE
REDS

Château Cos d'Estournel
2005 ($250)

Finca Allende
Aurus
2005 ($215)

Viñedos de Paganos
S.L. La Nieta
2006 ($150)

Château La Clémence
2005 ($110)

Campagnola Caterina Zardini
Amarone della Valpolicella Classico
2004 ($90)

MOST EXPENSIVE
WHITES

Verget Chablis
Les Clos
2006 ($84)

Ambullneo Vineyards
Big Paw Chardonnay
2006 ($60)

Ascheri
Montalupa Langhe Viognier
2004 ($48)

Radikon
Oslavje
2002 ($43)

Château Latour Martillac Blanc
2005 ($39)

TOP-RANKED
REDS

Château Cos d'Estournel
2005

Tishbi Estates
Jonathan Tishbi Special
Reserve
2004

Domaine Wardy
Private Selection
2006

Bucklin
Old Hill Ranch Zinfandel
2005

Boudreaux Cellars
Cabernet Sauvignon
2004

TOP-RANKED
WHITES

Luis Felipe Edwards
Gran Reserva Sauvignon Blanc
2007

Radikon
Oslavje
2002

Bénédicte de Rycke
Jasnières Cuvée Louise
2005

Topanga Vineyards
Grenache Blanc Celadon
2006

Domaine du Closel Château des Vaults
Savennières a Jalousie
2006

TOP-RANKED
AMERICAN

Bucklin
Old Hill Ranch Zinfandel
2005

Boudreaux Cellars
Cabernet Sauvignon
2004

Topanga Vineyards
Grenache Blanc Celadon
2006

Venge
Scouts Honor Red
2005

Rideau Vineyard
In-Circle Cellar Club Estate Viognier
2006

TOP-RANKED
IMPORTED

Château Doisy-Védrines
Sauternes
2005

Château Cos d'Estournel
2005

Luis Felipe Edwards
Gran Reserva Sauvignon Blanc
2007

Tishbi Estates
Jonathan Tishbi Special Reserve
2004

Radikon
Oslavje
2002

TOP-RANKED
SPARKLING

Françoise Bedel
Champagne Brut Entre Ciel et Terra
NV

Moët & Chandon
Dom Pérignon
1999

Rao's
Prosecco VSAQ Extra Dry
NV

Reymos
Espumoso de Moscatel
NV

J Vineyards & Winery
Cuvée 20
NV

TOP-RANKED
MERLOT

Château La Clémence
2005

Château Reignac
Cuvée Balthus
2005

Château Barde-Haut
2005

Clos des Moiselles
Le Bordeaux Merlot
2005

Paso Creek
Merlot
2005

TOP-RANKED
CHARDONNAY

Ambullneo Vineyards
Big Paw Chardonnay
2006

Verget
Chablis Les Clos
2006

Maison Louis Jadot
Pernand-Vergelèsses 1er Cru
Clos de la Croix de Pierre
2006

Monarchia Winery
Battonage Chardonnay
2006

Gunn Estate
Unoaked Chardonnay
2007

TOP-RANKED
PINOT NOIR

Domaine St-Nicolas
Fièfs Vendéens Cuvée Jacques
2005

Foris Vineyard & Winery
Rogue Valley Pinot Noir
Maple Ranch
2005

Lachini Vineyards
Estate Pinot Noir
2005

Ojai
Pinot Noir Clos Pepe Vineyard
2005

Arista
Russian River Valley Pinot Noir
2005

TOP-RANKED
DESSERT

Château Doisy-Védrines
Sauternes
2005

Dutschke
Sun-Raisined Shiraz

Domaine Imperial Hétszölo
Tokaji Aszú 5 Puttonyos
2001

Selaks
Premium Selection Ice Wine
2006

Rocca Bernarda
Picolit
2005

TOP-RANKED
CABERNET SAUVIGNON

Château Cos d'Estournel
2005

Boudreaux Cellars
Cabernet Sauvignon
2004

Hess Collection
Mount Veeder Cabernet Sauvignon
2005

Jocelyn Lonen Winery
Napa Valley Cabernet Sauvignon
2005

Anderson's Conn Valley Vineyards
Napa Valley Cabernet Sauvignon Estate Reserve
2005

TOP-RANKED
ITALIAN

Radikon
Oslavje
2002

Dievole
Chianti Classico Riserva Novecento
2004

La Gerla
Brunello di Montalcino Riserva
2003

Bartolomeo
Barolo
2004

Roagna
Opera Prima XV

TOP-RANKED
FRENCH

Château Doisy-Védrines
Sauternes
2005

Château Cos d'Estournel
2005

Bénédicte de Rycke
Jasnières Cuvée Louise
2005

Françoise Bedel
Champagne Brut Entre Ciel et Terra
NV

Clos Marie
Pic Saint-Loup Cuvée Simon
2004

TOP-RANKED
SPANISH

Cyclo
Christina
2005

Viñedos de Paganos
S.L. La Nieta
2006

Señorio de San Vicente
San Vicente
2005

Reymos
Espumoso de Moscatel
NV

Bodegas El Nido
Clio
2006

TOP-RANKED
AUSTRALIAN

Dutschke
Sun-Raisined Shiraz

Kilikanoon
Covenant Shiraz
2005

Pirie Tasmania
South Estelle
2006

Moondarra Vineyard
Holly's Garden Pinot Gris
2006

Fox Gordon
By George
2005

TOP-RATED
RHÔNE-STYLE RED BLENDS

Clos Marie
Pic Saint-Loup Cuvée Simon
2004

Domaine Gauby
Vieilles Vignes Rouge
2004

Domaine du Banneret
Châteauneuf-du-Pape
2005

Éric Texier
Côtes du Rhône-Villages Chusclan
2005

Edmunds St. John
Rocks and Gravel
2004

TOP-RATED
BORDEAUX REGION

Château Doisy-Védrines
Sauternes
2005

Château Cos d'Estournel
2005

Château La Clémence
2005

Château Reignac
Cuvée Balthus
2005

Château Haut-Bergey
2005

TOP-RATED
SOUTHERN HEMISPHERE

Luis Felipe Edwards
Gran Reserva Sauvignon Blanc
2007

Dutschke
Sun-Raisined Shiraz

Slowine
Rosé
2007

Kilikanoon
Covenant Shiraz
2005

Pirie Tasmania
South Estelle
2006

TOP-RATED
RED BLENDS

Château Cos d'Estournel
2005

Tishbi Estates
Jonathan Tishbi Special Reserve
2004

Domaine Wardy
Private Selection
2006

Bucklin
Old Hill Ranch Zinfandel
2005

Boudreaux Cellars
Cabernet Sauvignon
2004

WINES A-Z

INDEX

Underscored references indicate boxed text.

ACKNOWLEDGMENTS

Gosh, there are so many, and if I had to leave you out of this page I will thank you in person. First of all, one more thank you to my mom, who made me a star. My wife, for treating me like one. My sister, for being my first fan, and my bro, for being the next one. My dad, for always being one in his own way! I have to thank Bobby Shifrin, who is more then just a second cousin—he is a life-long friend. Brandon Warnke, for being my best friend for fifteen-plus years, and I know it will be for a hundred more! I also want to thank Erik Kastner for opening up new worlds to me. Without him there would be NO Wine Library TV. I want to thank Jon Malysiak for seeing what, at the time, some didn't, Rodale for being oh-so-smart and jumping on board, and Jeffrey Lindenmuth, for his amazing skills and friendship!